AFRICAN PROVERBS

WISDOM FROM ALL 54 NATIONS

Written In Their Native Tongues
With English Translations

MOTHERLAND LITERATURE

(Compiled By Bolia Tracey Nyemba)

"African Proverbs: Wisdom From All 54 Nations - Written In Their Native Tongues With English Translations"

Motherland Literature© 2023

www.motherlandliterature.com

@motherlandliterature

CONTENTS

INTRODUCTION

This book, a labour of love and a celebration of Africa's intellectual heritage, presents a collection of proverbs from every African country.

Thoughtfully selected by African writers, it stands as a testament to the rich linguistic legacy flourishing throughout the continent.

We extend our heartfelt gratitude to the countless individuals and communities across the 54 nations who have preserved and passed down these proverbs over time.

It is our hope that this book not only educates and engages but also fosters a deep appreciation for the languages, cultures, and wisdom that define Africa.

May "African Proverbs from All 54 Nations" serve as a testament to the enduring power of proverbs to illuminate our paths. Let us forever be guided by the wisdom of Africa's proverbs, and may their timeless insights enrich our lives.

ALGERIAN PROVERBS

Country: Algeria

Capital City: Algiers

Area of Country: 2,381,741km ^{2}

Population: 45,639,392

Demonym: Algerians

Currency: Algerian Dinar (DZD)

Independence Day: 5th July 1962

Official Languages: Algerian Arabic, Tamazight (Berber)

Other Languages Include: French

National Motto: By the people and for the people.

ABOUT ALGERIAN ARABIC

Algerian Arabic, also known as Darja or Algerian Dialect, is a dialect of Arabic spoken in Algeria. It is part of the Maghrebi Arabic dialect continuum, which includes similar dialects spoken in other countries such as Tunisia and Morocco.

ALGERIAN ARABIC - ENGLISH

1. **Serr tnin ya erfouh alfin** - A secret for two, soon a secret for nobody.

2. **Djouz aela el ouad el haddar ouala djouz aela el ouad essaket -** Cross the loud river but do not cross the silent one.

3. **Esberr maftah el djena** - Patience is the key to paradise.

4. **Li ma fi kerchou tben ma khaf mi nar** - The one whose belly is not full of straw is not afraid of fire.

5. **Koul klam elkhir ouala skout khir** - Speak kindly or refrain from talking.

6. **Lahna yegleb laghna** - Peace wins over wealth.

7. **El Yedd li tmedd khir men yedd li tchedd** - The hand which gives is better than the one which receives.

8. **Aeel laedaoua mzah** - There is an excess of familiarity at the root of all hostility.

9. **Hbibek min charkek fi lafrah oua laqrah** - A friend is someone who shares your happiness and your pains.

10. **Yedd ouahda ma tsafek** - One hand cannot applaud.

11. **Aedou aekel khir min sdik djahel** — A sensible enemy is better than a narrow-minded friend.

12. **Elli Khaff slem** - The one who shows his fear ensures his salvation.

13. **Laghrab habb yemchi mechyet lahmama nsa mechitou** - The crow wanted to mimic the pigeon's walk and forgot his own.

14. **Ki nchouf ham el nass nansa hami** - When I think of the other's misfortunes, I forget mine.

15. **El gayeb hedjtou maeh** - The absent always have justification.

16. **Aende echedda oua diq yadhar laedou min sdik** — A friend in need is a friend indeed.

17. **Wahed yahleb w lakhor chad lmahleb** - One person milks the cow and the other holds the cup of milk.

18. **Ma tjowaa dhib w ma tbeki raaiy** — Do not make the wolf hungry and do not make the sleeper cry.

3

19. **Moa wna teghleb s baa** – Together we beat the lion.

20. **Kol khanfous and mo ghzal** - Every beetle is a gazelle in the eyes of his mother.

21. **Kol taatila fiha khira** - The later, the better.

22. **El mehamia taghleb essbaâ** - Union means triumphs over the lion.

23. **Laklam lahlou yaldhaâ labba** - The soft tongue is sucked by the lioness.

24. **Aâlamnahoum slate sabkouna lahsira** - We taught them to pray, they got to the Mosque before us.

25. **Aïnek miszanek** - Your eye is the only way you can judge things.

ANGOLAN
PROVERBS

Country: Angola

Capital City: Luanda

Area of Country: 1,247,000km ^{2}

Population: 36,740,680

Demonym: Angolans

Currency: Angolan Kwanza (AOA)

Independence Day: 11th November 1975

Official Language: Portuguese

Other Languages Include: Umbundu, Kimbundu, Kikongo, Tchokwe, Ovambo

National Motto: Virtue is stronger when united.

ABOUT UMBUNDU

Umbundu, also known as Mbundu or Kimbundu, is a Bantu language spoken by the Ovimbundu people in Angola. It is one of the most widely spoken Bantu languages and is primarily used in the central and southern regions of the country.

UMBUNDU - ENGLISH

1. **Mbeu kalondi katchisingui, omanu vokapako** - A terrapin does not climb up a tree unless someone puts it there.

2. **Ehui lyamwile ovita** - The madman alerts by the imminence of war.

3. **O kauli wa tomba, oyo tu kuambata** – What you despise is what drives you.

4. **Nda ñgo kwasumbile usutu, sumba ñgo u olalemo** - If you do not respect the jungle, at least respect those who live there.

5. **Nda ilu lya otchipepi lambako** - While the opportunity lasts, take it.

6. **Ulika ukupanda ñgo osongo ko may kaukupi otchinene viso** - Alone you can remove a thorn from your foot, but you cannot blow a speck from your eye.

7. **Ukombe elende opita obamba** - A visit is like a passing cloud.

8. **Vomela yo sekulo vutunga ñgo eyo lyavola, kavutundi ondaka yavola** – A rotten tooth can come out from the mouth on an old man, but not a rotten word.

9. **Apa paswa vavali, paswa vatatu** - Where two can go, three can go.

10. **Tumala vondjali imosi, tuli ekuta** – Let us eat together, for we are children of the same father.

11. **Tchipepa tchipwa, tchivala tchilimba** - Good things end; pain fades away.

12. **Kahunlunkai nda olonga okanekulo kahe, ove okasipo yevelela** - If someone gives advice to your grandson, you who are standing beside him make the most of it.

13. **Kwatoko lukwene, likalyove tchikuponla** - Unity makes strength.

14. **Nda wamola kahañgo, katchiho kukawinasi** – Do not snub the old as you achieve the new.

15. **Ombolo ipepa yei tulitimbwila** - Delicious bread is shared bread.

16. **Ove kuyevayeva olondunge vyakulu, wenda la kasala** - Those who do not listen to their elders are doomed.

17. **Sindaka kaneñge, otcho henla kaneñge akusindikevo** - Take care of the child so that tomorrow the child will take care of you too.

18. **Epungu liwa konendela; omola sole kununulu** - Early corn is best, so the firstborn is the one to delight in it.

19. **Esalamiho liulume ka li enda enda no posi** - Labour has a sure reward.

20. **Etako lia muine omangu, utima ka wa muine omangu** – The body is easily satisfied but not the heart.

21. **Osikila wochila, opopela woyeva** – Play for who dances, speak to who listens.

22. **Apa wa lila omoma ka yu ku momenapo** – Full rewards of a deed are not reaped at once.

23. **Asuelela ka yukisa onganja** – Useless to cry over spilled milk.

24. **Ca fa ca topa; omalanga yi paplela vombandua yohosi** – The dead are no longer terrible.

25. **A wambata cilema tulatul, wakuyola okasi l'osande** – If you are carrying something heavy, rest slowly. Anyone who laughs is jealous of you.

BASOTHO PROVERBS

Country: Lesotho
Capital City: Maseru
Area of Country: 30,355km ^{2}
Population: 2,330,634
Demonyms: Mosotho (Sin), Basotho (Plu)
Currency: Lesotho Leti (LSL)
Independence Day: 4th October 1966
Official Languages: Sesotho, English
Other Languages Include: Isizulu, Siphuthi, Isixhosa, Afrikaans
National Motto: Peace, Rain, Prosperity

ABOUT SESOTHO

Sesotho, also known as Southern Sotho or Southern Sesotho, is a Bantu language spoken primarily in Lesotho. It is one of the 11 official languages recognised in South Africa.

SESOTHO - ENGLISH

1. **Tieho e tsoala tahleho** – Hesitation begets loss.

2. **Leboela ha le ngallwe** - You may succeed where you once failed.

3. **Meso e tswala meswana** - Procrastination is the thief of time.

4. **Noka e tlatswa ke dinokana** - The river is filled by the streams.

5. **Imbewu ihlalela ihlanga layo** - Each seed waits for its time to be sowed.

6. **Pere e wa e ena le maoto a mane** - To err is human.

7. **Tlaila le tlailela morena** - Do not be afraid to make mistakes so that they may be corrected.

8. **Mejo ha e rutanwe, ho rutanwa ditlhare** - Every man is the architect of his own fortune.

9. **Tlaila le tlailela morena** - Do not be afraid to make mistakes so that they may be corrected.

10. **Ngoana mahana a joetsoa o bonoa ka hkhapha** - If you do not listen you will always cry.

11. **Moiketsi ha a llelwe** - He who rejects advice deserves no sympathy.

12. **Mohana ho jwetswa o tshohela leomeng** - A word is enough for the wise.

13. **Leboela le a ja** - Perseverance pays.

14. **Pinyane ha e senye motse** - It is wise to keep certain things secret.

15. **Dithoto ke lefa la ba bohale** - Fools are stepping stones of the wise.

16. **Ditabana di tswala ditaba** - Mighty things rise from trivial ones.

17. **Taba di mahlong** - The face is the index of the mind.

18. **Botswa ha bo jelwe** - Laziness does not pay.

19. **Moketa ho tsoswa o itekang** - God helps those who help themselves.

20. **Sejo-senyane ha se fete molomo** - Half a loaf is better than no bread.

21. **Pitsa ho fahwa e belang** - The pot that boils receives attention.

22. **Pula ke mahiopha a senya** - Rain does good and harm.

23. **Leleme ha le na malokeletso** - The tongue has no fastenings.

24. **Ditabana di tswala ditaba** - Small talk gives birth to big talk.

25. **Leraba le tshwasa ya le tjhehileng** - A trap catches the one who set it for others.

BENINESE PROVERBS

Country: Benin

Capital City: Porto-Novo

Area of Country: 114,760km ^{2}

Population: 13,731,373

Demonyms: Beninese, Beninois

Currency: West African Franc (XOF)

Independence Day: 1st August 1960

Official Language: French

Other Languages Include: Fon, Bariba, Yom, Yoruba, Gen, Kabiyé, Tammari, Fulfulde

National Motto: Fellowship, Labour, Justice

ABOUT FON

The Fon language, also known as Fongbe or Fon-Gbe, is a member of the Gbe language group, which is part of the larger Niger-Congo language family. The Fon language is primarily spoken in the southern region of Benin. It is also spoken by communities in neighbouring countries such as Nigeria and Togo.

FON – ENGLISH

1. **Xogɔ̀ zanfɔ̀n nɔ̀ gɔ̀ gbadà a** - Being satisfied in the morning does not mean that one will be satisfied until evening.

2. **Ayi we nö kɔ̀n sukpö nyú** - One can never catch a fly by acting without sagacity.

3. **E kpɔ̀n nu gbannya gbannya nyönaxo tɔ̀n ɔ̀, e na xwle zö xi a** - If one focuses on an old man's scowl, one will not shop at a distant market.

4. **Xan é ma yon sé a é non dji do min si non koho ta haa** - One does not sing a song that is not good to hear in the courtyard of one's mother-in-law.

5. **Awasagbe mö ajinakú fö lobo ðekɔ̀ : e sí me ðé nukún me ɔ̀, e nö le sí gudó tön** - A squirrel bows before the footprints of an elephant and says: we should respect a person in his absence as well.

6. **Dosú gudunö klen afö bo j'ayi : e ðö gbe kpo ðo nukön** - The leper stumbled, fell to the ground, and said: life goes on.

7. **Agluzagbo gba dekín gbön tögbadome bö ðegbó nyi kö bo kpɔ̀n e : lan jö lan ðé we nye ve dó** - The pig breaks palm nuts in the bed of a river and attracts the eyes of the hippopotamus which says: I thought I was in the presence of a much larger animal.

8. **Nya ðé dɔ̀ xove bö ayihɔ̀n be le gön gleta : kan yí do kanjí we a ðè** - A man sleeps hungry and does not go to the farm the next day: will he rise in rank?

9. **Nya ðé gbo kpentin do blo azakpo ná : nu e àyi ðéwu é ðe nɔ̀ gblé a** - A man used a papaya trunk to make the ceiling of his room: your environment is useful in all things.

10. **E nye awön ðo ahwlikpönuwa gɔ̀n bo kpɔ̀n gudo : nu e a na ko wa do nukön ɔ̀, e we a wa gbön gudo** - A man passed wind in front of a beautiful woman without looking behind him. That is what he should have done in the first place.

11. **Nyönú ðé klɔˋdokwín bö asú tɔ̀n be yi sa. Nuklɔ̀sá h án me ðé a** - A woman washed potatoes, and her husband was quick to go sell them. Everyone has something to value.

12. **Anuwanumɔ̀nɔˋtafö abla ma ji ðò axijije me. Ye kó sɔˋðú sín me xóxó** - A fool trampled an empty package of bean donut in the market. They ate it long ago.

13. **Anuwanumɔ̀nɔˋmö ajotɔˋðo gle le we : ene nyɔˋhu ðe ɔˋ** - A fool sees an old thief cultivating a field and says: This method is better than stealing.

ABOUT BARIBA

The Bariba language, also known as Baatonum, Bariba-Ben, or Baatombu, is a Gur (Voltaic) language spoken by the Bariba people in parts of Benin, Togo, and Nigeria. It is a member of the larger Niger-Congo language family, specifically within the Gur branch.

BARIBA – ENGLISH

14. **À n kperun tim kí a ku wunæn gbáan nøø mææri** - If you want honey from a stone, do not fear the blade of your axe.

15. **Bóø ga ku ra gen buu døm gu ka kúkuru turi** - A dog does not bite its puppy to the bone.

16. **Ba à n Gusunø sokuu, a n ka dáa næni** - When invoking God, hold on well to the branch.

17. **Turo waaru, søndara** - The gain of only one (person) is a failure.

18. **À n ka sii bura, a ka sii nø** - If you eat with others, you must drink with others.

19. **Wì u ku ra tii wí, bisi wíira ta ra nùn go** - He who does not criticise himself, dies from the critiques of others.

20. **Wì u kusunu yiru gira, sansa u ra yare di** - Someone who runs after two partridges at the same time only catches feathers.

21. **Wì u yaamø, u ku ra n yä win** - Whoever dances is unaware that their bottom is bent.

22. **Guroguro kùn ka bii yabebuu wáa** - The clothes of a child do not fit an adult.

23. **À n gisø yä, a ± sia yä** - If you now know today, you do not know tomorrow.

24. **À n næǽ googii u ku sí, wunægii ku ra kabiri** - When you say that someone else's child will not walk, then yours will not crawl.

25. **Baa nim køsum mù ku ra garu ko, mu ra dóø go** – Even though dirty water seems useless, it can at least be used to extinguish fire.

BISSAU - GUINEAN PROVERBS

Country: Guinea-Bissau

Capital City: Bissau

Area of Country: 36,125km ^{2}

Population: 2,153,204

Demonym: Bissau - Guinean

Currency: West African Franc (XOF)

Independence Day: 24 September 1973

Official Language: Portuguese

Other Languages Include: Guinea-Bissau Creole (Kiriol) , Badyara, Bainouk-Gunyuno, Balanta-Kentohe, Bassari, Bayot

National Motto: Unity, Struggle, Progress

ABOUT GUINEA-BISSAU CREOLE (KIRIOL)

Guinea-Bissau Creole, often referred to as Kriol (or Kiriol), is a creole language spoken in Guinea-Bissau and neighbouring regions of Senegal and Gambia. It as a lingua franca among the country's diverse ethnic groups.

GUINEA-BISSAU CREOLE (KIRIOL) – ENGLISH

1. **Baga baga i ka ten tarsadu, ma i ta korta paja** - The termite does not have a machete, but it cuts grass.

2. **Baka misti korda, i ka tenel, kabra tenel, tok i na rasta** - The cow wants rope but does not have it; the goat has it but drags it.

3. **Bardadi i suma malgeta: i ta iardi** - The truth is like a chili: it burns.

4. **Bariga pode debu o debu ma bu ka ta toma faka bu rumpil** - No matter how bad the belly is, you do not cut it with a knife.

5. **Bianda di kaleron ka ten dunu** – Food in the pot has no owner.

6. **Bias bu ta sibi dia di bai, ma bu ka ta sibi dia di riba** – When travelling, one only knows the day of departure, but not the day of return.

7. **Bibus na cora, ki-fadi mortus** – If the living cry, what about the dead.

8. **Boka ficadu ka ta ientra moska** – Flies cannot enter a closed mouth.

9. **Bolta di mundu i rabu di punba** – The circles that the world takes are like the wings of a dove.

10. **Bunitasku di iagu salgadu i bunitu, ma i kansadu bibi** – The beauty of salt water is great, but it is unpleasant to drink.

11. **Dinti mora ku lingu, ma i ta daju i murdil** – The teeth live with the tongue, but sometimes they bite it.

12. **Dun du caga ka ta sinti fedos di si pe** – People with foot odour cannot smell their own feet.

13. **Firminga ka ta janti, ma i ta ciga** – The ant does not take the lead, but it arrives.

14. **Piskadur k' torkia si kanua pa kabalu, i sibi ke k' manda** – The fisherman who exchanges his canoe for a horse knows why.

15. **Mon pa mas que grandi e ka na tapa ceu** – No fist is big enough to hide the sky.

16. **Sancu nega papia pa ka paga dasa** – The monkey does not talk as to not pay tax.

17. **Tataruga kuma si pe i kurtu ma i ta lebal tudu kau ki misti** - The turtle says its legs are small, but it takes it where it wants.

18. **Uju ka ta kume, ma i kunsi kusa sabi** – The eye does not eat but knows what is tasty.

19. **Ñambi iasadu, i ka sabi sibi si ta kusidu** – You never know if the roasted yam is well cooked.

20. **Korda ta kansa kabra, ma i ka ta matal** – The rope ties the goat but does not kill it.

21. **Baga-baga i ca ta cata iagu, ma i ta massa lama** - Termites do not fetch water but produce mud.

22. **Galinha cargadu ca sibi si caminhu i lundju** - The transported hen does not know the length of the way.

23. **Cobra cuma riba tras ca ta quebra costa** - The snake says that when he looks back he does not break his back.

24. **Fork of pis i iagu** - The strength of the fish is water.

25. **Prague by buru i ca ta subi na sèu** - The curses of the donkey do not ascend to heaven.

BOTSWANA PROVERBS

Country: Botswana

Capital City: Gaborone

Area of Country: 581,730km ^{2}

Population: 2,677,602

Demonyms: Motswana (Sin) Botswana/Batswana (Plu)

Currency: Botswana Pula (BWP)

Independence Day: 30th September 1966

Official Language: English

National Language: Setswana

Other Languages Include: Kalanga, Kgalagadi, Shona, Mbukushu, Ndebele, Tshwa

National Motto: Rain

ABOUT SETSWANA

Setswana, often referred to as Tswana, is a Bantu language which is spoken by roughly 78% of the Botswana population as a first language. It is also an official language in South Africa as well as spoken in Zimbabwe, and Namibia, where it is known by different names, including "Sechuana" and "Sechwana."

SETSWANA – ENGLISH

1. **Eetshetlayana etsala eerunneng** - A poor cow can give birth to a fine calf.

2. **Lesilo galeke leboela nnyo gabedi** - The fool does not return to the virgin twice.

3. **Sedibana pele goseikangwe** - The well ahead is not reliable.

4. **Maru gasepula mosi kemolelo** - Clouds and smoke may be similar, but clouds do not mean rain just because smoke means fire.

5. **Tshwene ebonye mapalamo, mafologo gaeabona** - The baboon found the way up, but could not find the way down.

6. **Osetshege yooweleng mareledi asale pele** – Do not laugh at the fallen for the slippery path is still ahead.

7. **Ketlaja gasekejele, kejele keyoomompeng** - "I shall eat", is not "I have eaten"; "I have eaten" is which that is in the stomach.

8. **Alaano gaasitwe gosita aloso** - Plans protect, but not against death.

9. **Legwatagwala labasimane nna kgolo reboya dinao** - The race of the young is not entered by the old.

10. **Mmatla kgomo kotlomela oetse mhata sediba** - One who seeks a cow should go as deep as the digger of a well.

11. **Monna legapu obutswetsa kafateng** - Man is like the melon, the interior ripeness is not visible.

12. **Ntshanyana ebonwa mabutho boton** - A dog shows that it will become a hunter by running around as a puppy.

13. **Dijo morwa tshalo boramoratiwa** - A man of much food always has company.

14. **Ntsi eokwa keboladu** - Flies gather on a wound.

15. **Se nkganang se nthola morwalo** – What rejects me also reduces my burden.

16. **Balsomi gabaka ballhakanelwa sekgwa** - Hunters will never be satisfied in the same forest.

17. **Sejo sennye gasefete molomo** — (Even) a small amount of food does not pass by the mouth.

18. **Bobalabala gangwana gasebotlhale** - A child who talks much is not necessarily clever.

19. **Mojaboswa gaagake** - The heir is always recognisable by his actions.

20. **Ga go lekanwe go se meno** — People are not equal unlike teeth.

21. **Mmatla kgwana gaarobala** - One who seeks a red cow with white spots does not sleep.

22. **Boferefere gasepapadi** - There is no profit in cheating.

23. **Seila kgaka se nwa moro** — People do not always turn out to be what they say.

24. **Thukwi erile kelebelo motlhaba ware kenamile** - The aardwolf said, "I am fast" and the sand said, "I am wide".

25. **Ngwana yoosautlweng molao wabatsadi outlwa wamanong** - A child who does not listen to its parents' warning is heard by the vultures.

BURKINABÉ PROVERBS

Country: Burkina Faso

Capital City: Ouagadougou

Area of Country: 274,200km ^{2}

Population: 23,281,237

Demonym: Burkinabé

Currency: West African Franc (XOF)

Independence Day: 5th August 1960

Official Language: French

National Language: Mooré, Bissa, Dyula, Fula

Other Languages Include: Mande languages, Gur languages, Senufo languages

National Motto: Unity, Progress, Justice

ABOUT MOORÉ

The Mooré language, also known as Mossi (Moré, Moreng), is a Gur language spoken by the Mossi people in Burkina Faso, Ghana, Ivory Coast, and Togo.

MOORÉ – ENGLISH

1. **To saoog n dɪkda, to zʋg ka rɪkd ye** - You can copy someone else's dance, not their flaws.

2. **Zĩrẽ zoeta yʋʋm tusri, tɪ sɪd wa yõk-a raar a ye** - In a day's run, the truth outweighs the lie on its thousand-year run.

21

3. **Sēn togs-a zõang ma kʋʋr n gãt-a nugu** - He who announces the funeral of a blind man's mother will be responsible for leading him there.

4. **Pʋg rʋmd ka mi t'a sɪd yaa naab ye** - A chief's sweetheart has no regard for his greatness.

5. **Ki n boond noaaga** - It is grains that attract the hen.

6. **Ned sã n kẽnd kiu-kiu, bɪ a tẽeg lama-lama yelle** - If someone walks with big steps, because he is strong, he must think of the days when he will walk with small steps, for lack of energy.

7. **Ned tõeeme n tɪ baa gãande, la a ka tõe ta a muma nin ye** - You can force a dog to lie down but not to close its eyes.

8. **Bi-bɛɛg sã n be ra-poore, a to n be nin-taore** - The fearless from the East had better know that there is another in the West.

9. **Wʋm tɪ lar kʋʋd yẽbga, ka rɪkd n lob koomẽ ye** - If it is true that with an axe you can kill a caiman, it is not by swinging it in the water.

10. **Ned sã n ka ki, bɪ a ra sõda yẽn ye** - As long as you live, it is useless to count your teeth.

11. **Yẽnd sã n ya a ye, bɪ a yɪ pɛɛlga** - If someone has only one tooth, at least let it be clean.

12. **Kɪm sã n pãb ned yʋngo, a ges-a-la wĩntoogo** - Before attacking a person at night, the ghost first took a good look at him during the day to find out if he would be able to.

13. **Ra wa-m yiri, yaa ra wa-m yiy a yiibu** - By prohibiting a person from coming to your home, remember that at the same time, you are denying yourself access to their home.

14. **Koadeng yeelame tı yõor la gɛla** - The partridge says: protecting your eggs is good but protect yourself first.

15. **Yibeoog saag sã n ka wa ne boɛɛga, zaabr saag na wa ne-a** - If the morning rain fails to bring a goat back into the pen, the evening rain will bring it back.

16. **Fo sã n yã ned ne a rıgẽ bãaga, ra yet-a kõn ta beoog ye** - If you see someone suffering from a disease for a year, do not tell him that he will die of it before tomorrow.

17. **Ned mıı-a tõẽta laa ka mia kʋʋd ye** - Who is stronger than you, you know; but who can kill you, you do not know.

18. **Pãng sãn tũũd sore, bʋʋm bʋta moogo** - When force takes a path, reason goes behind.

19. **Sugr soab yaa Wẽnnaam zoa** - Who knows how to forgive is friends with God.

20. **Sũ-keelem la wãbre, yẽn gãee yaa zaalem** - To crunch you need courage, not long teeth.

21. **Wãbr ne fılg ka naagd taab ye** - You cannot chew and whistle at the same time.

22. **Ninsaal maan neere, n wiligd a nedlem** — It is the good actions of a man that attest to his human value.

23. **Soaamb ka nobd n yiig a gaong ye** - A hare does not grow bigger than its skin.

24. **Senyood- yaad ka oet kiims yabr ye** - Whoever walks in cemeteries cannot complain or be afraid of the cries of ghosts.

25. **Wẽnnaam ka kõt nag-tãadg yıl ye** - God does not give sharp horns to bulls that like to charge.

BURUNDIAN PROVERBS

Country: Burundi

Capital City: Gitega

Area of Country: 27,834km^2

Population: 13,257,022

Demonym: Burundian

Currency: Burundian Franc (BIF)

Independence Day: 1st July 1962

Official Languages: Kirundi, French, English

National Language: Kirundi

Other Languages Include: Swahili

National Motto: Unity, Work, Progress

ABOUT KURUNDI

Kirundi, also known as Rundi, is a Bantu language spoken primarily in Burundi. Kirundi is also spoken in neighbouring countries like Rwanda, Tanzania, and the Democratic Republic of Congo (DRC), where it is used by Burundian refugees and migrant communities.

KIRUNDI - ENGLISH

1. **Akanyoni katagurutse ntikamenya iyo bweze** - A bird cannot know where the sorghum is ready (to be eaten) unless it flies.

2. **Intrinda irandura** - He who is not careful gets contaminated.

3. **Impene mbi ntuyizirikako iyawe** - You do not tie your goat to a bad goat.

4. **Ubana na suneba ugasuneba nka we** - When you stay with a careless person, you end up becoming careless just like him/her.

5. **Akagabo karaje ukuguru hanze kitwa Imburanmutima** - A man who spends his leg outside (his house) is called "Heartless".

6. **Burira ntibutera ku mpeshi** - The night does not last until the good season.

7. **N'iritagira inkoko riraca** - A night without roosters will still end.

8. **Igiti kigororwa kikiri gito** - A tree is straightened while it is still young.

9. **Inahasi y'umutindi yamubujije kwiyahura** - The unlucky man's hope prevented him from committing suicide.

10. **Ivya gusa bitera ubwenge buke** - Free things decrease one's intelligence.

11. **Amazi masabano ntamara imvyiro** - Water aid does not completely remove the dirt.

12. **Aho ishari ritari agashato ka Rukawavu gakwira bane** - Where there is no jealousy, a small hare's leather is enough to cover four people.

13. **Aho Uburundi butunze urutoke hubakwa inzu** - Wherever Burundi points a finger, a house is built.

14. **Isinzi ntibesha** - The crowd does not lie.

15. **Nta witamga Imama kwihebura (guhebura)** - You do not give up to despair before God.

16. **Wanka bangwe ntiwanka zana ndabe** - You refuse to stop fighting but you cannot refuse to show the wounds/consequences.

17. **Umanika agatu wicaye mu kukamanura ugahaguruka** - You can hang an item from where you are seated but when you want to take it down you must stand up.

18. **Ikiza kitaguhitanye kiraguhitaniza** - When an epidemic does not kill you, it gives you some benefits.

19. **Ntawurya akatamugoye** — No sweet is made without effort.

20. **Uwutazi umuti awubishako** - He who does not know medicine defecates on it.

21. **Uwanka agakura abaga umutavu** - He who hates growth kills a calf.

22. **Nta wutera atengase** - You cannot throw something while you are holding many others.

23. **Uburo bwinshi ntibugira umusururu** - Many millet grains do not make porridge.

24. **Amayira abiri yananive imfyisi** - It has been always difficult for a hyena to go through two different paths (at the same time).

25. **Pha-balimo o ja le bona** - A person who gives to the ancestors, eats with them.

CABO VERDEAN PROVERBS

Country: Cape Verde

Capital City: Praia

Area of Country: 4,033km ^{2}

Population: 598,988

Demonyms: Cabo Verdean, Cape Verdean

Currency: Cape Verdean Escudo (CVE)

Independence Day: 5th July 1975

Official Language: Portuguese

National Language: Cape Verdean Creole (Kriolu)

National Motto: Unity, Work, Progress

ABOUT KRIOLU

Cape Verdean Creole developed because of the complex historical and cultural interactions between African, European (primarily Portuguese), and to some extent, indigenous languages. Kriolu is a vital aspect of Cape Verdean culture and identity.

KRIOLU - ENGLISH

1. **Odju más grandi ki stangu** - The eye is bigger than the stomach.

2. **Katxor ki ta ladra ka ta morde** - Dogs that bark do not bite.

3. **Katxor sumuladu ta morde rixu** - Quiet dogs bite the hardest.

4. **Mau kaminhu ka ta leba bon lugar** - Bad ways do not lead to good places.

5. **Pior surdu é kel ki ka kre obi** - The worst deaf person is the one who does not want to listen.

6. **Makaku ka ta djobe se rabo** - A monkey does not look at its own tail.

7. **Fidju kabra tudu ta ba rótxa** - All Billy goats know how to climb rocks.

8. **Orédja más bedju ki txifri** - Ears are older than horns.

9. **Saku baziu ka ta sakedu** - It is hard for an empty bag to stand upright.

10. **Dentu di algen ki é algen** — It is what is in you that makes you human.

11. **Pensa ku sabedoria, más papia ku sinplisidadi** - Think with wisdom and speak with simplicity.

12. **Kenha ki ta obi, ta odja** - The one who does not listen, will see.

13. **Korbu ta bua na altura má, é na txon ki el ta kume** - Crows fly high, but they eat on the ground.

14. **Algen ku korason linpu ka ta fronta** - Someone with a pure heart will never suffer.

15. **Tudu sinbron tem direitu a se góta di agu** - All sons and daughters deserve their blessings.

16. **Panéla bedju ki ta kusia sabi** - Old pans cook the most delicious foods.

17. **Kenha ki ta riklama txeu di bida, ka ten ténpu di vive** - Those who only complain about life do not have time to live it.

18. **Un mon ki ta laba kel out** - One hand washes the other.

19. **Un ómi di idadi ta sta más pértu di se téra y un maridu di idadi ta sta más pértu di se mudjer** - An aging man gets closer to his land and an aging husband closer to his wife.

20. **Nu pode gengi más nu ka ta kai** - We might bend but we will not fall.

21. **Ka ten ninhun spedju midjor ki bu midjor amigu(a)** - There is no better mirror than a best friend.

22. **Ómi sen mudjer é sima vazu sen flor** - A person without a spouse is like a vase without flowers.

23. **"N sabe tudu" ka ta dexa bedjera di prende faze mel** - "I know it perfectly" prevents the bee from learning to make honey.

24. **Galinha ta anda sô ku un pé, óras ki el sta na un lugar nóvu** - The hen walks on one leg in new surroundings.

25. **Kenha ki ta fla verdádi ta koredu ku el di tudu kau ki el pasa** - Whoever tells the truth is chased out of nine villages.

CAMEROONIAN PROVERBS

Country: Cameroon

Capital City: Yaounde

Area of Country: 475,442km ^{2}

Population: 28,687,305

Demonym: Cameroonian

Currency: Central African Franc (XAF)

Independence Day: 1st October 1961

Official Languages: French, English

Other Languages Include: Bamileke Languages, Ewondo, Bassa

National Motto: Peace, Work, Fatherland

ABOUT BAMILEKE (FÈ'ÉFĚ'È)

Fe'efe'e also spelled Fefe or Fe'fe' is a language spoken primarily in the town of Bafang and its surrounding areas in the West Region of Cameroon. It is one of the Bamileke languages, which collectively belong to the larger Bantu language family within the Niger-Congo language family.

BAMILEKE (FÈ'ÉFĚ'È) – ENGLISH

1. **Wèn baňŋɑ' ó nkabừɑ' ì ǒ sì thí kə' tú ì** - If someone carries you on the shoulder, do not take his head.

2. **Kwě' wèn sǐ' mbɑ̄ nshừ' à lāh mmɑ' sừū bɑ̄** - If you have a single spear, refrain from throwing it at the elephant.

3. **Lǐ' zhwìē wèn mɑ̀ ǎ mɑ̀mfǎm nshì mɑ̀ ó yá' lǎt nshì mbī'tū mɑ́** - Before making fun of someone who is drowning, you should have already crossed the river.

4. **Móó mbɑ̄ nkòó mɑ̄ ā, ǎ lɑ̀ zhī mɑ́ nzhǐ sàh** - When a child is on his mother's back, he does not know that the road is long.

5. **Wèn hòó pò' zǐ ndòm lòh, ǒ sì ghén ntɑ' kò** - If someone harvests his mushroom on a rock, do not go and search the fields.

6. **Lēn yǒ mbú í mɑ́ nhòò fēn sǐ' mbɑ̄ nkò' nɑ̄h bɑ̄ mbī'tū mɑ́** - Tell him that the one who finds is not necessarily the one who has big eyes.

7. **Pō shù̀' sǐ' nkwāt pū' bɑ̄** - With one hand, you cannot tie a bundle.

8. **Nshǐ mfhū̄ ntɑ'ntɑ' tɑ̄ ndōh tū̄ɑ̄** - Water comes from several sources before filling a container.

9. **Nkə'nǐ mbɑ̄ ndū̄ɑ̄ pó lɑ̀ zhī ngà'mbōk** - When there is love in a house, we do not distinguish the poor.

10. **Nkə'nǐ shù̀ɑ̄ nkɑ̄ɑ̄** - Love is beyond money.

11. **Lǐ' mɑ̄nnū ndù' mɑ́ nnū nshì mbī'tū mɑ́** - When drinking wine, you must also drink water.

12. **Ò mɑ̌mbōh nàh njēē nzhù̀ ǒ sì dīē** - If you are afraid to have nightmares do not sleep.

13. **Yò wèn mɑ́ thú shū̄ɑ̄ mɑ̀ ǒ nzɑ̄ yò nò' mɑ̀ yáá sēn** - If you know someone with a plum tree, you will eat dark (well ripe) plums.

14. **Tɑ' wěn sì láh kòlə' kò nkɑ' nā ì** - However, we must not count on a plantain (diet) that is in the field.

31

15. **Wèn sǐ' nzhī nò' nzǖ kɑ́ nhɑ̄ mvāt lɑ́ bɑ̄** - We do not know the palm nut that produces oil.

16. . **Wèn lɑ' khúɑ́ mbàk ngwɑ' nshwī** - You do not flee the rain by throwing firewood.

17. **Pó nzhī mbā' ndéndēē mɑ́ ntìè' ē sēē** - It is in the rainy season that we recognise a real man.

18. **Wèn lǎk sìpè' à nū mǒ' ntū'** - If you learn to do harm, part of this evil will come back to you.

19. **Mēmmɑ̄ ò, ò tìé mɑ ǒ nkɑ̄ɑ̄** - My brother - if you sow, you will reap.

20. **Wūɑ̄kɔ' mbɑ̄ ngwɑfʉ̀ɑ̀** - Death is blind.

21. **Ngèn kò ndìàndìà sǐ' mbɑ̄ ndə' bɑ̄** - The one who regularly goes to the field is not a sloth.

22. **Wū lɑ' kwéé mbóm. Ngwá' ntōm mvǎt pōk** - Two events never coincide favourably: when you have salt, you run out of oil.

23. **Ǒ mɑ̄njók nnəə̀ púɑ́ nkwéé nsəə̄** - If you hunt two animals at the same time, you will lose both. Who hunts two hares does not get one.

24. **Fùfùà yì ǎ nŋɑ' nthū lɑ́ sǐ' nkéé sāk nàh mfūā bɑ̄** - The wind that blows the trees does not prevent the birds from flying.

25. **Mbè' wú mbɑ̄ sǐ' nshūɑ̄ kò** - Every good thing is at the end of the forest.

CENTRAL AFRICAN PROVERBS

Country: Central African Republic
Capital City: Bangui
Area of Country: 623,000km ^{2}
Population: 5,751,596
Demonyms: Central African
Currency: Central African Franc (XAF)
Independence Day: 13th August 1960
Official Languages: Sango, French
Other Languages Include: Ngbandi, Banda Languages, Sara Languages
National Motto: Unity, Dignity, Work

ABOUT SANGO

Sango, also known as Sangho, is a creole language spoken primarily in the Central African Republic. It is based on the Ngbandi language of northern Democratic Republic of Congo. Sango is also spoken in neighbouring countries like Chad and South Sudan.

SANGO-ENGLISH

1. **Zo so a gne bia na mo ake mou na mo tene, ma ni si** - A person who sings for you gives you a message, listen to it.

2. **Zo so mo na la a te la aveke zedou ti koua ti mo** - The one you eat with is the one who digs your grave.

3. **Zo so a gne a zo akpe lo a linkpi lo kpe tere ti lo ozo ni si** - Respect yourself first and you will be respected.

4. **Zo tinzingo mbo ake de na lo ti bagara ape** - There is no difference between a dog thief and a cow thief.

5. **Zo so a mou kete a on zo ti anda** - A person who gives you a little is better than the one who promises you.

6. **Za sit ere ti mo a zele pepe tongana da ti ita ti mo a gbi** - Do not rejoice when your neighbour's house is burning.

7. **Waziba a pe ti gboto mba ti lo waziba ape** - A blind person cannot assist another blind person to walk.

8. **Tongana mo inga ndo so mo goue da pepe, bando na peko ti gueret ti mo** - If you do not know where to go, look at where you come from.

9. **Tongana ye ondoni na yati da, zoni ye ayeke doutingo kpon** - When quarrels persist, silence is the best solution.

10. **Tongana mo ke tene na molengue pepe, mo gne lo pepe** - If you do not correct your child of anything wrong, you do not love them.

11. **Tongana legue ni a ba, da ni ayeke ninga pepe** - When the foundation of the house is curved, the house will not last.

12. **Tongana gola a koui, ake tanga ti kando pepe** - When a king dies, it is not the end of the kingdom.

13. **Tongana e yeke na da ousse, gui tie eyek nde** - When you have two homes you become unstable.

14. **Tongana ngoongo a mou na mo maboko ba foungo tit ere ti lo pepe** - If an eagle assists you in travelling fast do not complain about the smell from its wings.

34

15. **Te kete mo bata tangani tene ti kekereke** - Eat a little and save for tomorrow is another day.

16. **Siriri a dou nan do so tatene ake da na bira nan do so vene ake da** - Peace reigns where there is truthiness while war is the fruit of lies.

17. **Sala mbeto na zo na kate ti mo pepe, nzapa la a mouni na mo** - Never boast due to your chest, it is God who gave it to you.

18. **Ngou so a do pepe ake mene zo** - A river without waves and storms, is that which swallows people.

19. **Ngui a ken a zo so a ma tene na bata** - Goodness is for a person who listens and preserves.

20. **Ndeke a fa le kobe pepe na lo wara tit e lakouet** - A bird does not farm but still gets food.

21. **Na ti kodoro so a wato ti mo a yeke da, zo ti yengo mo nga a yeke da** - In a village full of your enemies, you never lack a friend.

22. **Mo ke ko longo ti ye so mo la mo lou** - What you sow is what you harvest.

23. **Maboko oko a gbou siri na li pepe** - A hand without support cannot get victory.

24. **Kongo na makassi ake fouta nan do guigui lakouet** - Patience and courage pay in life.

25. **Bamara ake kirika na peko pepe** - A lion cannot walk backwards.

CHADIAN PROVERBS

Country: Chad

Capital City: N'Djamena

Area of Country: 1,284,000km ^{2}

Population: 18,309,815

Demonym: Chadian

Currency: Central African Franc (XAF)

Independence Day: 11th August 1960

Official Languages: French, Arabic

Other Languages Include: Teda, Ngambay, Dazaga, Zaghawa

National Motto: Unity, Work, Progress

ABOUT TEDA

Teda, also known as Tedaga or Daza, is a Nilo-Saharan language spoken by the Teda people primarily in the Tibesti Mountains region of Chad. This region is in the northern part of Chad, near the border with Libya.

TEDA – ENGLISH

1. **Agurnun gubia tedîe daamoó, êgishi ye** - If you do not want your contemporary to get ahead, give him a loan.

2. **Shin cubin, soun cubunnodi bozú** - One who eats the ear will not rest without eating the eye.

3. **Aũ kandama čusčinã, sa hunã kôi di wûni hûdu čûwo mannu, čudurú** - Someone chasing after profit does not see a fire burning between his feet.

4. **Yunu agur numaa-ã̄ dogusu tigiriĩ, numaa dûski tigiri** - What happens to your contemporary during the night can happen to you in broad daylight.

5. **Aũ hananummãá, yunu hananummó yida** - A person that you do not know has something that you do not know.

6. **Gînei di gûi tugopoo, dûli di ashi curuuwo gali** - When we slit the goat's throat improperly, it is important to skin it properly.

7. **Goni hi gûndunú, kûruni hi hunaktunú** - One cannot hide on a camel, and one cannot conceal one's footprints in the sand.

8. **Aba murdom yidado, ba murdom yidannó yugó** - There is no one who has ten fingers who does not have ten relatives.

9. **Wûni yê adibi yê, turo, kunu yugó** - There is no such thing as a small fire or a small woman.

10. **Gaŋanũwo anna buĩ, kinennũwo bapa buĩ** - If you hurry, you will eat something unripe, but if you are patient you will eat what is ripe.

11. **Yuhadu njennaán ha mêdi yeún! Turci njennaán ha labana yeún** - To the one who does not support you in speech, do not give him a word; to the one who does not watch out for you, do not confide in him.

12. **Wûroei nôushi gunu** - Protecting oneself or being careful is not the same thing as being afraid.

13. **Agur numa bûdugi-ĩ hi bûni čiledoo mannu, hallu yiled** - If your rival digs a well through the rock, you dig one too.

14. **Aũ ôrozi njenã̄, tumo wuniši nje. Aũ wur njenã̄, kînjigi nje** - Someone who gives you possessions has given you a night of sleep, someone who gives you advice has given you a way to make a living.

15. **ALLA wor, môši wor** - God is powerful, a neighbour is powerful.

16. **Anna čû tîrize: njidaú njennãá yê njidaá durrinjinnãá yê** - Two people are equal: one that likes you but gives you nothing and the other that does not like you but does you no harm.

17. **Naizanu du horkusu benii togo nũwo, togo hunu yida** - If you put off today's work until tomorrow through laziness, tomorrow has its tomorrow.

18. **Aũ ALLA galayunã čičilko, čîidi aũ galayunã buumsu** - Someone who is counselled by God is clear-sighted, but someone who is counselled by a person is unmindful.

19. **Haraũ ko tuyumbĩ gunnoó, kiši toyumbú** - Ill-gotten gains fill the mouth but not the stomach.

20. **Kudur kudurčunoo, šidenu tôlti yoguri** - If it is destined to be, a fly will break a water jar.

21. **Kaaši yê sôdorki yê turo, sudura mundu** - Someone who has lived a long life and someone who listens well are one: each knows a lot.

22. **Kandama zondu gunú; kubor zondu** - Ambition is not bad; taking an oath is bad.

23. **Kĩnnimmi aũ njeni; bui-ĩ ALLA njeni** - People give small things; God gives big things.

24. **Kiši ndenno numa kiši ndenno hunu yida** - Whomever you talk to in confidence, he has his own confidant.

25. **Ko waktunnó di tumo čuruú** - Without opening the mouth, a tooth will not come out.

COMORIAN PROVERBS

Country: Comoros

Capital City: Moroni

Area of Country: 2,235km ^{2}

Population: 853,062

Demonyms: Comorian, Comoran

Currency: Comorian Franc (KMF)

Independence Day: 6 July 1975

Official Languages: Comorian (Shingazidja Dialect, Shimaore Dialect, Shindzwani Dialect, Shimwali Dialect), French, Arabic

Other Languages Include: Bushi, Malagasy, Maore Comorian

National Motto: Unity, Solidarity, Development

ABOUT COMORIAN (SHINGAZIDJA DIALECT)

Comorian, specifically the Shingazidja dialect, is one of the languages spoken in the Comoros. Comorian is a Bantu language with various dialects spoken on the different islands of the Comoros archipelago. Shingazidja, also known as Shingazija, is one of the primary dialects and is spoken primarily on Grande Comore (Ngazidja), the largest island of the Comoros.

COMORIAN (SHINGAZIDJA DIALECT) – ENGLISH

1. **Mipango itsona nyaswia ka ikamilishiha** - Failure follows plans which lack counsel.

2. **Mipango itsona nyaswia yo ufuba, amma eilona marandrazi yo uwadi** - Plans lacking counsel will fail, but the one with advisers will arrive.

3. **Yafikiri haye ce hafikiri na shetwani** - He who thinks alone, thinks with a devil.

4. **Alimao juaju atsola mvulini** - The one who farms in the sun will eat in the shade.

5. **Mntru mlalamishi katabu wakati walazimu, na uwakati wa mavuna waye utsaha be kapara** - A sluggard does not work his land when he should and at harvest time he looks and finds nothing.

6. **Hazi de mdzade wa litumo** - Work is the mother of gain.

7. **Fitina ndo sumu yah'emaesha** - Gossip is the poison of life.

8. **Roho nyimakinifu yo uburudisha ziungo, sha uvu wo uwolesa ziba** - A peaceful heart refreshes the body, but envy rots the bones.

9. **Matso male kayana baraka** - Envious eyes do not see blessings.

10. **Oufahari wa shababi nd'ezenvuu zahahe, sha le truru la mndru-mduhazi nd'ezenvi zahahe** - A young man's glory is his strength and grey hair is the splendour of the old.

11. **Mndru-mduhazi ye ushindwa mbio sha ye kashindwa âkili** - You can beat an old man in a race, but not in knowledge.

12. **Mndru kadotunda ezilio honyumani** — Do not stick your nose in the latrine.

13. **Eundiio baya latsumhusu, ye hama nd'euzingaro m§wa emashishio ndziani** - One who jumps into someone else's fight, is like a man who grabs a stray dog by the ears.

14. **Mkabaya wapvahasiwa ha mbondzi ndraru wo uhomo rubuha** - A braid of three chords makes a durable rope.

15. **Mnyongo mdzima ka upveye** - A broom of one branch cannot sweep

40

16. **Mndrumshe mwema tsi suraya** - A wife's beauty is not on the surface.

17. **Daho kuu tsi ndezempado** - The greatness of a home is not its structure.

18. **Mndru wa ndrazini ye ubarikishiha eka nguhanyiso eriziki yahahe ndaye n'emamaskini** - Blessed is a generous person because he shares his food with the poor.

19. **Fikira mbili zo uzava lulu** - Two minds yield treasure.

20. **Mndru mmakinifu yeona âdjali ehwitrawa, sha emdjinga ehwitsenglea n'ivo humlilia nayi** - A sensible person sees danger and avoids it, but a fool draws near and it ends badly.

21. **Emwendza twamaya nd'eulona muo, ba hata m§wa vendza muo yo kairi rahana simba yahafa** - The one who has hope is the one who is alive, because even a live dog is better than a dead lion.

22. **Dji la mdzima ka litukua ngono** - One voice cannot create a harmony.

23. **Ndjema kaziwolo** - Good does not rot.

24. **Emdjinga yetsodjiona na haki. Amma, emwendza hikma eushilia zenyaswia** - The way of a fool is straight in his own eyes, but a wise person listens to advice.

25. **Evambiwa âkili vaishia hakana mbapvi** - The one who is imparted knowledge and listens gains knowledge.

CONGOLESE PROVERBS (DRC)

Country: The Democratic Republic of Congo

Capital City: Kinshasa

Area of Country: 2,344,858km ^{2}

Population: 102,475,706

Demonym: Congolese

Currency: Congolese Franc (CDF)

Independence Day: 30th June 1960

Official Language: French

National Languages: Lingala, Kikongo, Tshiluba, Swahili

Other Languages Include: Mongo, Sango, Zande, Bangala

National Motto: Justice, Peace, Work

ABOUT LINGALA

Lingala is a Bantu language spoken in several countries of Central Africa, with its primary speakers residing in the Democratic Republic of the Congo, especially in the capital city, Kinshasa. It is also spoken in the Republic of the Congo, the Central African Republic, and Angola, among other places.

LINGALA – ENGLISH

1. **Molinga ebimaka pamba te** - Smoke does not come out for nothing

2. **Monoko epesaka nkolo monoko makambu** - The mouth gives its owner problems.

3. **Mosala na mosala ezali na lifuta na yango** – Each job has it is pay.

4. **Tuta ebende ntango ezali na moto** - Strike the iron when it is hot.

5. **Soki olukaka makambo, okozua** - If you are looking for trouble, you will find it.

6. **Soki okolie makei, koboya soso te** – If you ate eggs, do not reject the chicken.

7. **Nzambe alalaka te** – God does not sleep.

8. **Ntango ozali na mino, buka mokua** - While you have teeth, break bones.

9. **Lala na ndaku nde okoyeba esika mbula etangaka** - Sleep in the house then you will know where the rain falls.

10. **Zoba liboso, mayele na sima** - Stupidity first, then intelligence.

11. **Bato ya mawa ekatisaka ngambo te** – A boat of pity never makes it across.

12. **Ata moto ya mbongo akoki kodefa mungua** – Even a rich person can borrow salt.

13. **Bolamu tosalaka awa na se ekofutamaka kaka awa nse** – The good we do here on earth will be paid to us here on earth.

14. **Monduki ezanga masasi elelaka te, kasi motema oyo ezanga bolingo, elelaka bilelalela** – A gun without bullets does not make noise, but a heart which lacks love makes noise by continuously crying.

15. **Mutu ya lokuta ye na ndoki mutu moko** – A liar and a sorcerer are comparable.

16. **Muselekete alekaki ndaku na ye likola ya kokima mbangu** — The lizard passed his house due to rushing.

17. **Mosapi moko esukolaka elongi te** — One finger does not wash the face.

18. **Mbisi alandaka esika mayi ezo tshola** — The fish follows the water flow.

19. **Keba na esika ya kobuaka mposo ya etabe, ekoki kokweisa yo** — Be careful where you throw your banana peel, it can cause you to slip.

20. **Mokili ezali mbanga ya ntaba** — The world is a goat's jaw.

21. **Banga makambu, makambu ekobanga yo** — Be afraid of problems and problems will be afraid of you.

22. **Mayi eninganaka pamba te** — Water does not move for no reason.

23. **Mbongo ezalaka na suka te** — Money has no end.

24. **Lilala moko ya kopola epolisaka malala nionso** — One rotten orange rots all oranges.

25. **Mokili ekendaka liboso, kasi ezongaka sima te** — The world moves forward but not backwards.

CONGOLESE PROVERBS

Country: The Republic of Congo
Capital City: Brazzaville
Area of Country: 342,000km ^{2}
Population: 6,115,658
Demonym: Congolese
Currency: Central African Franc (XAF)
Independence Day: 15th August 1960
Official Language: French
National Languages: Lingala, Kikongo
Other Languages Include: Monzombo, Kilari
National Motto: Unity, Work, Progress

ABOUT KIKONGO

Kikongo, also known as Kongo or Kikongo ya leta, is a Bantu language spoken in Central Africa. It is primarily spoken in the Republic of the Congo, the Democratic Republic of the Congo and Angola, with some speakers in other neighbouring countries.

KIKONGO - ENGLISH

1. **A engi adilanga mu longa se adila va makaya, ay'adilanga va makaya se adila mu longa** - He who eats on a plate, will sooner or later eat on leaves.

2. **Alambi ayingi madia avivisanga** - Too many cooks spoil the soup.

3. **Ambote i akwendanga, ambi-i asalanga** - Good people go and bad ones remain.

4. **A tuma avava, anati a nsangu a engi** - Bad news travels fast.

5. **Avo nti watekama yana kwa mbangu kasingika, elongi dia mbote muntu a mbote uvananga dio** - If a shrub is crooked, give it to an expert to straighten it.

6. **Avo tota ntumbu mu nzila, muntu vitidi mo sotwele yo** - If you find a needle along your way, there is someone who arrived before you and placed it there.

7. **Avo wele vata, wene wantu atei fma, ngeye mpe telema, avo avwanda, ngeye mpe vwanda** - When entering a village, if you find people standing up, stand up too; if they are sitting, you also sit down.

8. **Awole wantu, umosi ninga** - Two persons are people, one (person) is a shadow.

9. **Kana kala ngeye mosi, yuvula mbundu aku. Avo a ole luna luyuvudyana** - If you are alone, take counsel of your pillow. If you are two, put heads together.

10. **Kitantu ka kina ye longo ko, nanga loloka ye loloziana** - Hate has no cure, except forgiveness.

11. **Bunda ntulu, ntulu woboka** - To beat one's chest as a sign of arrogance is to bruise one's chest.

12. **Dilu ka myuluzi ko** - Weeping does not save, and sadness does not make it any better.

13. **Dya kana kutuka mpaka, mazowa adidi ko** - If the meal causes a quarrel, it is a signal that those who cat it are fools.

14. **Dya kwa mene, makani nkokela** - He who wants to eat in the morning, must prepare it the night before.

15. **Dya lunda, nzala lumvutu** - Bat and spare, because hunger will come back.

16. **Dya lunda toma kwatoma** - To eat and to keep something for tomorrow is foreseeing.

17. **Dyambu dyambote dilenda kituka se dya mbi eadya mbi dilenda kituka se dya dya mbote** - By its use, a good thing may become bad and a bad one may become good.

18. **Dyambu kadiloswangwa ko. Walosa dyo mu maza, kadikukula ko. Walosa dyo va tiva, ka divya ko** - You cannot get rid of a problem without solving it. If you throw it into the river it will not flow away, or if you throw it into fire, it will not get burnt.

19. **Ezi zikokolanga ku maki zitukanga** - The roosters that sing began as eggs.

20. **Ivitidi ku nkoko katekanga myunzu ko** - He who arrives first to the spring does not drink troubled water.

21. **Ka mamona umosi ko** - A difficult situation is not the fate of one sole individual.

22. **Kana bakama mu koko, lenda vuluka, kana bakama munwa vonzai** - If you are caught by your arms, you can escape, but if you are caught by your mouth, it is dangerous.

23. **Kana kiwana, dila kyo** - If something of good occurs in your lifetime, reap profit from it.

24. **Kana baka sengo a mpa, ekudi kulozi ko** - If you have a new hoe, do not throw away the old one.

25. **Kana zaya kesa, zaya venga** - If you know to cut down trees, be cautious to avoid them when they fall.

DJIBOUTIAN PROVERBS

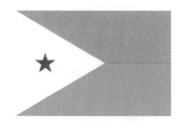

Country: Djibouti

Capital City: Djibouti

Area of Country: 23,200km ^{2}

Population: 1,137,555

Demonym: Djiboutian

Currency: Djiboutian Franc (DJF)

Independence Day: 27th June 1977

Official Language: Djibouti Arabic, French

National Languages: Afar, Somali

Other Languages Include: Monzombo, Kilari

National Motto: Unity, Equality, Peace

ABOUT AFAR

Afar, also known as Afar Af, is a Cushitic language spoken by the Afar people primarily in the Afar Region of Djibouti, Ethiopia, and parts of Eritrea. It is one of the Afroasiatic languages, specifically belonging to the Cushitic branch within this language family.

AFAR - ENGLISH

1. **Able kal mayxiganay atce kal mayanxuqaana** - You do not know what you do not see, and you do not swallow what you do not chew.

2. **Labha malisek warri akiyybaxiiy yanbulleh** - A small ant can destroy a large termite mound.

3. **Caxa naba caxa haada garrissah numuk naba num cami garrissa** - A big tree is surrounded by birds as a big person is surrounded by gossip.

4. **Yoh xic yemeggek anaakar yamaggeh anaakar yemeggek hawi tamagge** - The one who knows does not talk, and the one who talks does not know.

5. **Caal kee corod caba iyyanamah macaban** - Bad personality and bad body posture cannot be corrected at will.

6. **Akke wayni ma yakkaay, danan laa ma kora** - The impossible remains the impossible, a donkey cannot breed a cow.

7. **Afiyyem taanam gactaah bagi maaqo cinam gacta** - Wisdom is not like wealth that can be inherited.

8. **Abaluk ruubeenim able kalah gunnusan** - Today's negligence brings the fruit of regret.

9. **Yab yaabal geyaanah buxa ascossil geyan** - Speech is found by speech as a house is found by the direction others give.

10. **Ku tegen koh rabah marin gundul kariyta** - The scorpion is not strong against the bite of a snake.

11. **Yab ceela mara leeh yaabah lafta mari yan** - There are people with good speech who should speak as there are people speedy to talk ill.

12. **Yab yab ceelak koo yaysammeh daco lee ceelak koo taysamme** - A seemingly good-natured speech may cause dispute as urine may seem like water and may cause harm.

13. **Yab maggo num garayak caban dalwa maggo barra xalak caban** - An ill-intentioned person is secluded from discussion, as an adulterer woman gives birth but is not included into a family.

14. **Yab waanam qadadaay can waanam qadowwaya** - A lack of speech causes dullness as a lack of milk causes Gadowwaya. *(Gadowwaya is an illness caused by a lack of calcium.)*

15. **Missili missila ceelam meqeeh baxi abba ceelam meqe** - A proverb must look like a proverb as a child should look like his father.

16. **Aben yab dan faxah xalen baxi can faxa** - What you speak needs a good confidant as much as a newborn needs milk.

17. **Ardak kala aban gexo tan gadwa kal aban yab yan** - There is a walk that is not running as there is a talk that is not singing.

18. **Sidiicakel malse ke sidiica numulih mala baahi** - The fool is known by his foolishness.

19. **Malisse makaban temeetek malse wayte makaban af mutuc hayta** - Those who come after discussion among themselves talk sense but those who come with no prior discussion have no fruitful idea to tell.

20. **Yab gita leeh qari afa lee** - Speech has a way as a house has a door.

21. **Yab elle yanimil mayaabanay baaxo elle tanimil magexan** - You do not say all you have heard just as you do not walk all roads.

22. **Yab koo yaxeeh lee koo beytah** - A promise is convincing, as a river takes you by force.

23. **Abte gaba baytaamah, gaba abtem ma bayta** - The author is gone, the fruits of his labour remain.

24. **Akat eleelem yaarreeh, gaba eletem tacee (tabbixe)** - A rope is used according to its length.

25. **Addalekket aban yab yaniih addalekket kalan xogorti yan** - Trust no one, not even yourself.

EGYPTIAN PROVERBS

Country: Egypt

Capital City: Cairo

Area of Country: 1,002,450km ^{2}

Population: 126,747,211

Demonym: Egyptian

Currency: Egyptian Pound (EGP)

Independence Day: 28th February 1922

Official Language: Arabic

National Languages: Egyptian Arabic

ABOUT EGYPTIAN ARABIC

Egyptian Arabic, also known as Egyptian Colloquial Arabic or Masri, is the spoken variety of the Arabic language that is widely used in Egypt. Egyptian Arabic is a regional variety of Arabic, and like other Arabic dialects, it is part of the larger Semitic language family. It differs significantly from Modern Standard Arabic (MSA), which is the standardised form of Arabic used in formal contexts.

EGYPTIAN ARABIC – ENGLISH

1. **it-tikraar yi3allim il-Humaar** - Repetition teaches (even) a donkey.

2. **il-waHda xeir min giliis is-suu'** - Being alone is better than being with a bad person.

3. **iT-Tuyuur 3ala askaaliha taqa3u** - Birds of a feather flock together.

4. **illi 3ala raasu baTHa biHaSSiS 3aleiha** - Those who have an injury on their head keep checking it.

5. **iid waHda matsa"afš** - One hand does not clap.

6. **3ala 'add liHaafak midd regleik** - Stretch your legs as far as your blanket extends.

7. **anta turiid wa-howa yuriid wallaah yaf3al ma yuriid** - You want what you want, and he wants what he wants, but God does what he wants.

8. **il-3ein mate3laaš 3al-Haagib** - The eye does not go higher than the brow.

9. **Tabbaax is-simm biyduu'u** - One who cooks poison tastes it.

10. **il-Haraka baraka** - Movement is a blessing.

11. **ig-gayyaat aHsan min ir-rayHHaat** - What is coming is better than what is gone.

12. **is3a ya 3abd wana as3a ma3aak** — Make an effort and I'll make an effort to help you.

13. **il-gahl ni3ma** - Ignorance is bliss.

14. **il-'offa omm widnein yišiiluuha tnein** - A basket has two handles for two people to carry it.

15. **ta'ti r-riyaaH bi-ma la taštahi s-sufun** - Winds do not blow as the ships wish.

16. **SaaHib balein kaddaab, wa-SaaHib talaata mnaafi'** - Someone who tries to do two things at once is a liar, and someone who tries to do three things at once is a hypocrite.

17. **in sara't, isra' gamal, wa'in 3eše't, i3ša' 'amar** - If you steal, steal a camel, and if you love, love someone as beautiful as the moon.

18. **kulle muškila wa-liiha Hall** - Every problem has a solution.

19. **il-i3tiraaf bil-Ha"e faDiila** - Admitting when someone else is right is a virtue.

20. **is saa3i fil-kheir ka'faa3ilu** - The person seeking to do good is as good as someone who does it.

21. **riHlit il-alf miil tabda' bixaTwa** – From small beginnings come great things.

22. **illi bi-yiigii hinaak bi-yruuH hinaak** – What comes this way, goes this way.

23. **Dawaam il-Haal min il-muHaal** – Continuing the same state is impossible.

24. **Fil-imteHaan yokram il-mar' aw yohaan** – When tested, a person rises or falls.

25. **biyiTla3 Id-Daww biduun SiyaaH id-diik** – Dawn breaks (even) without the crowing of the cock.

EQUATORIAL GUINEAN PROVERBS

Country: Equatorial Guinea

Capital City: Malabo

Area of Country: 28,051km ^{2}

Population: 1,717,467

Demonym: Equatorial Guinean

Currency: Central African Franc (XAF)

Independence Day: 12th October 1968

Official Languages: Spanish, French, Portuguese

Other Languages Include: Fang, Bube, Annobonese Creole, Kombe, Kwasio

National Motto: Unity, Peace, Justice

ABOUT FANG

Fang, also known as Fang-Ntumu, is a Bantu language spoken by the Fang people primarily in Central Africa, specifically in parts of Equatorial Guinea, Gabon, and Cameroon.

FANG – ENGLISH

1. **Nge o sup kup o gnél nfiang** - It is good to be satisfied with soup in the absence of chicken meat.

2. **Ke vuene bi lè amu alu e ndang ayap** - Do not forget the dream because the night was long.

3. **Abâm e ne bômo ochiñ mimbu ntet e se ki venghan koas** - A piece of wood can stay in the river, but it will never turn into a fish.

4. **M'aben mitié asse na mene atak** - Seeking peace is not a sign of weakness.

5. **Ayong d'a wulu ya agnep** - Solidarity is the strength of a people.

6. **Minenga a ne owore otong** - A woman is like a source that does not dry up.

7. **Alu da da bole dia zock** - An elephant does not rot in one night.

8. **Kiri ngueng, mame ngeng** - In the morning everything is illuminated.

9. **Bim ônoane ede duma** - The size of the nest corresponds to that of its bird.

10. **Moan kup a wu, da daghe moan soa ové** - The chick is killed, the duckling does not take it into account.

11. **Kulu a nga vare dang nkoa gne ne za a biñ gne** - The turtle unable to cross the piece of wood on his way asks who is holding him back.

12. **Melep ma kome zing** - Too much advice causes animosity.

13. **Bindeng bi koup bia sole gne okote** - The chicken hides her thinness under his feathers.

14. **Mone kabane a dzi elok ngnie ads** - The little goat eats the same grass that his mother eats.

15. **O yéne fe kup da kobo alu, o edzok e ne gne abé** - The chicken does not shout at night for nothing.

16. **Nneng a yem ve song, a yem kig é môt a ne ô song si** - The stranger notices the presence of a tomb but does not know the one buried there.

17. **Ze da kulu kig byèn kagha na a bin** - The panther does not bring out its claws before jumping on its prey.

18. **Alu dã da'a bwèlè zokh** - The elephant's corpse cannot decompose in a day.

19. **Y'a bo na nge nkagha a kpwé' öswin be nã a manang melelang** - The iguana does not lose the stains of its skin because it fell into the river.

20. **Öswin ö nga wulu nkwat amu kagha nlere zen** - In the absence of advice, the river ended up with meanderings.

21. **Ôndôndoe a se mongo nsama bikyèn** - The needle is not negligible in the mist of steel objects.

22. **Önyu vogho ke va'a fwas e mbil** - A single finger cannot remove a palm worm from its hole.

23. **Bebèn ökang é se avuman** - Proximity is not synonymous with kinship.

24. **É moan a nga baghela nnöm énye a nga nong medo** - It was the child who took care of the old man that inherited his knowledge.

25. **É dzam nyamôrô â yén a to'o ô si, na mongo a yen do, à téré a tebe, â vere ntén** - What the wise man sees sitting, the young person, to see, must get up and stand on their tiptoes.

ERITREAN PROVERBS

Country: Eritrea

Capital City: Asmara

Area of Country: 117,600km ^{2}

Population: 3,761,511

Demonym: Eritrean

Currency: Eritrean Nakfa (ERN)

Independence Day: 24th May 1993

National Languages: Tigrinya, Tigre, Kunama, Bilen, Nara, Saho, Afar, Beja

Other Languages Include: Arabic, English

ABOUT TIGRINYA

Tigrinya is an Afroasiatic language spoken primarily in Eritrea. Within Afroasiatic, it is classified as a Semitic language, specifically an East Semitic language. Tigrinya is also spoken by a significant population in neighbouring Ethiopia, particularly in the Tigray region and among the Tigrayan people.

TIGRINYA – ENGLISH

1. **ኩሉ ስጋ ኣብ ኣፍ ኩሉ ሰብ ሓደ ኣይኮነን** - All meat is not the same in every man's mouth.

2. **ኣቐዲሙ ዝተገመተ ሓደጋ ፍርቂ ይውገድ** - A danger foreseen is half avoided.

3. **ድሌት ኣብ ዘለዎ መንገዲ ኣሎ** - Where there is a will, there is a way.

4. **ኩሉ መፍረዪ ማይ ናብ ናይ ገዛእ ርእሱ መፍረዪ ማይ ይስሕብ** - Every miller draws water to its own mill.

5. **ሓጺርነት ነፍሲ ብልሒ እዩ** - Brevity is the soul of wit.

6. **ኑዛዜ ቀዳማይ ስጉምቲ ንስሓ እዩ** - Confession is the first step to repentance.

7. **ምዝራብን ምግባርን ክልተ ነገራት እዩ** - Saying and doing are two different things.

8. **ምዕጉርቲ ዓወት የምጽእ እዩ** - Cheek brings success.

9. **ኣብ ሽግር ዘለዎ ማያት ጽቡቕ ምግፋፍ ዓሳ እዩ** - It is good fishing in troubled waters.

10. **ካብ ዓቢ ሓዊ ዘቃጽለና፡ ንእሽተይ ሓዊ ንምቖና ይሓይሽ** - Better a little fire to warm us, than a great one to burn us.

11. **ካብ ስቅ ዝበለ ከልቢን ስቅ ዝበለ ማይን ተጠንቀቚ** - Beware of a silent dog and still water.

12. **ብዘይ (ገላ) ረሃጽ ምቁር የለን** - No sweet without some sweat.

13. **ናይ ነፍሲ ወከፍ ሰብ ጌጋ ኣብ ግንባሩ ኣይተጻሕፈን** - Everyone's faults are not written on their foreheads.

14. **ሰነፍ በጊዕ ሱፋ ከቢድ መሲልዋ** - A lazy sheep thinks its wool is heavy.

15. **ዋላ ሓንቲ ከይገበርና ሕማም ክንገብር ንመሃር** - By doing nothing we learn to do ill.

16. **ጽቡቕ ኣሚንካ ጽቡቕ ኣለካ** - Believe well and have well.

17. **ብዘይ ገላ ንእሽቶ መኽሰብ ዓቢ ክሳራ የለን** - No great loss without some small gain.

18. **ኣብ ሓጺር ግዜ ይፍጸም** - Self done is soon done.

19. **ድሕሪ ዝናብ ርትዓዊ ኩነታት ኣየር ይመጽእ እዩ** - After rain comes fair weather.

20. **እቲ ዝጸልመተ ሰዓት ቅድሚ ወጋሕታ እዩ** - The darkest hour is that before dawn.

21. **ቅድሚ ምዝላልካ ምዝላል ተማሃር** - Learn to creep before you weep.

22. **ዓሽ ኮለል ይብል ለባም ይጓዓዝ** - The fool wanders, the wise man travels.

23. **እቲ ብገንዘብ ንኣምላኽ ዘገልግል ንድያብሎስ ብዝሓሸ ደሞዝ ከገልግሎ እዩ** - He who served God for money will serve the devil for better wages.

24. **ኣድላይነት ኣደ ምህዞ እያ** - Necessity is the mother of invention.

25. **ፈጺሙ ዘይፈሽል ፈጺሙ ኣይሃብትምን እዩ** - He who never fails will never grow rich.

ETHIOPIAN PROVERBS

Country: Ethiopia

Capital City: Addis Ababa

Area of Country: 1,112,000km ^{2}

Population: 127,127,108

Demonym: Ethiopian

Currency: Ethiopian Birr (ETB)

Freedom Day: 5th May 1941

Official Languages: Amharic, Afar, Oromo, Somali, Tigrinya

Other Languages Include: Sidamo, Wolaytta, Gurage, Hadiyya, Gamo, Harari

ABOUT AMHARIC

Amharic is a Semitic language spoken predominantly in Ethiopia. It is one of the world's oldest languages with a rich linguistic history and cultural significance. Amharic is written in the Ge'ez script, also known as Ethiopic.

AMHARIC – ENGLISH

1. **ዛፍ ያለቅርንጫፍ አይደምቅም ሰው ያለሰው አይከበርም** - A tree does not shine without a branch; a person does not shine without a person.

2. **ነብር አይኑን ታመመ ፍየል መሪ ሆነ** - The tiger's eyes hurt and the goat became the leader.

3. **ዛሬ የትላንት ነገ ከበረች ዛሬ ደግሞ የነገ ትላንት ትሆናለች** - Today was yesterday's tomorrow and today will be tomorrow's yesterday.

4. **ዛብ የሌለው ፈረሰኛ ምሳ የሌለው ኮሰኛ** - A rider without a saddle is a rider without lunch.

5. **ዝምታ ራሱ መልስ ነው** - Silence itself is an answer.

6. **ባለቤትያከበረውአህያበቅሉይለውጣል** - The donkey that the owner respects grows and changes.

7. **ዝምታ ወርቅ ነው መናገር ብር ነው** - Silence is gold, speaking is silver.

8. **ዝባድን ከውሻ እምነትን ከባላጌ አትሻ** - Do not ask a dog for a dog's faith.

9. **ዛር ልመና ሳይያዙ ገና ከተያዙ ብዙ ነው መዘዙ** - The consequences are many if you are caught without asking.

10. **የለመኑትን የማይረሳ የነገሩትን የማይረሳ** - Never forget what you asked, never forget what you said.

11. **የለመነ ያገኛል የነገደ ያተርፋል** - He who begs gets, he who trades gains.

12. **ነብር ቢያንቀላፋ ዝንጀሮ ጎበኘው** - If a tiger sleeps, a monkey visits him.

13. **ነውር ለባለቤቱ እንግዳ ነው** - Shame is a stranger to its owner.

14. **ነገሩ ነው እንጅ ቢላዋ ሰው አይጎዳም** - The thing is, a knife does not hurt a person.

15. **ሲሾም ያልበላ ሲሻር ይቆጨዋል** - He who does not eat when he is appointed will be punished when he is revoked.

16. **ቃል መግባት እዳ ነው** - A promise is a debt.

17. **ለመኖር ብላ እንጂ ለመብላት አትኑር** - Live not to eat but eat to live.

18. **ይጥበብ መጀመሪያ እግዚአብሔርን መፍራት ነው** - Wisdom is fearing God first.

19. **ጌጥያለቤቱቄምጥናነው** - Study without decoration.

20. **ሰውእንደቤቱእንጂእንደጉረቤቱአይተዳደርም** - A man is not governed by his house, but by his neighbour.

21. **መንገድየምታውቅአይጥከፈረስየበለጠትሮጣለች** - A mouse that knows the way runs faster than a horse.

22. **የዘሩትሁሉአይበቅልም፤የወለዱትሁሉአያድግም** - Not everything you sow will grow, not everything you give birth to will grow.

23. **ግብፃችለአበሻደግሰውላይሰጡ** - The Egyptians did not give up.

24. **አንድዓይንያለውበአፈርአይጫወትም** - A one-eyed man does not play in the dirt.

25. **በፈረስየፈለጉትበእግርይገኛል** - What you want on horseback can be found on foot.

62

GABONESE PROVERBS

Country: Gabon
Capital City: Libreville
Area of Country: 267,668km ^{2}
Population: 2,445,649
Demonym: Gabonese
Currency: Central African Franc (XAF)
Independence Day: 17th August 1960
Official Language: French
Other Languages Include: Myene, Punu, Fang, Mbete, Teke, Villi,
Nzebi
National Motto: Union, Work, Justice

ABOUT MYENE

The Myene language, also known as Mpongwe or Mpongwe-Myene, is a Bantu language spoken by the Myene people in Gabon, Equatorial Guinea, and parts of the Republic of Congo and Cameroon.

MYENE – ENGLISH

1. **Ombɔma n'ombɔma w'amɛname** - Python's do not swallow each other.

2. **Ike nyi njɔghɔni a revhuni ngyɛ** - The hen's egg advised its mother.

3. **Gho tar'inyomba, ko wa dyivir'owɛndɛ** - To be the head of the family, you must be able to accept humiliation.

4. **Ogheningo a gɛndi rego kɔndɛnɛ édɛng'oma wi tevuna yɛ** - The river took detours because it found no one to guide it.

5. **Ikaza nyi ngani e dyóngino** - You do not take the test of poison in someone else's place.

6. **Nkula mori mori ye dyoniz'otondo** - We fill the basket nut by nut.

7. **Iyano nyi ngwɛ mori nyi zele ni mbɛmi n'ogara** - When two brothers argue, neither of them should be right.

8. **Ntondo yere ni njina ye re dulo gh'ozo** - One does not speak ill of a person in the presence of one of his relatives.

9. **Mbuwe a ze n'igholo** - The clan is priceless.

10. **Nkema né djiv'ilonda, djina né bonguinya yo** - The monkey picks the fruits, the gorilla eats them.

11. **Ebongune ntende, ere nye mbile ntende** - Whoever grows a young palm tree, does not eat the fruit.

ABOUT PUNU

The Punu language, also known as Ikwa or Yipunu, is a Bantu language spoken by the Punu people in Central Africa, primarily in Gabon and the Republic of Congo.

PUNU – ENGLISH

12. **Ikume ama vio pangini** - Chance is better than promise.

13. **Mondi makulu mane, nzile mossi** - The dog has four legs, but all four follow the same direction.

14. **Isantsu muponsi befuli imo imosi** - The wood from a basket is unloaded one by one.

15. **Dilungu éghobi na tsande, kingu, éghobi na musang, dibal éghobi na mughétu** - The waist is beautiful because of the loincloth, the neck is beautiful because of the necklace, the man is respected because of a wife.

16. **Dirangi aghé djiéghili ghiari imosi** - The buttock does not dance on one side.

17. **A bamabe bak tsingul basamabe** - Those who were, must tell those who were not.

18. **Tsoli dji purumughi kedi, duvangu mukolu** - The bird that flies by day prepares for the night.

19. **Mondi aghé burili va misu ma fumu** - A dog does not give birth in front of its master.

20. **Dusombi aghékési matsi, mutu tsing aghékési ubwédji** - The palm worm does not boast of being fat and the human person does not boast of being beautiful.

21. **Dilawu, pa amavul tsande, ik wivuli djiawu, djiénu botsu ik malawu mabédji** - If a madman abandons a loincloth and you also abandon yours, you both look crazy.

22. **Dilongi aghé basi ponzy** - A piece of advice does not fill the basket.

23. **Dinong polu** - Friendship is good health.

24. **Iso babedji ilatse mbatsi na nsale** - A property that belongs to two is likely to deprive one of its benefit.

25. **Aghi dugu ndagu ghilu madil aghe dugu ndagu** - Sleep always fills a house which is not the case with wealth in a house.

GAMBIAN PROVERBS

Country: Gambia

Capital City: Banjul

Area of Country: 11,300km ^{2}

Population: 2,786,146

Demonym: Gambian

Currency: Gambian Dalasi (GMD)

Independence Day: 18th February 1965

Official Language: English

Other Languages Include: Mandinka, Wolof, Pulaar, Serer, Jola, Fulani

National Motto: Progress, Peace, Prosperity

ABOUT MANDINKA

Mandinka, also known as Manding or Mandingo, is a Mande language spoken by the Mandinka people in West Africa. It is one of the major languages within the Manding sub-group of the Mande language family. The Mandinka language is spoken in several West African countries, including Gambia, Guinea, Senegal, Mali, Guinea-Bissau, Sierra Leone, Liberia, and Ivory Coast. Mandinka is spoken as a first language for 38% of the Gambian population.

MANDINKA – ENGLISH

1. **Nana buka boi banko to kensenke** - The swallow does not come down to the ground for nothing.

2. **Yiri dima, hani n'a selo kuyata, ka fending jolong** – Even if climbing a fruit tree is difficult, it lets something fall.

3. **Dolo-bato koto, a buka a sunkango bo** - An old palm wine calabash does not lose its smell.

4. **Kacha meringo ka larang koto fengo bondi** - A long chat brings out things hidden under the bed.

5. **I ye suo siti, I mang nyo di a la** — You have tied up the horse, but you have not given it any millet.

6. **I bulo kono nyeo, kana a bula i sing koto nyeo ye** — Do not leave the fish in your hand for the fish under your foot.

7. **Kantarla ye a la bolo mabo dameng, a buka doko fai je** - Where the herdsman has put away his gourd, he does not throw a stick in that direction.

8. **Kumo kuntu ka kelo tariya** - Abrupt talk (talk cut short) hastens fighting.

9. **Mo buka fo bambo ye tuneng** - A person does not tell a crocodile how to dive.

10. **I namanang kelo balang, i si sonko balang** - Before you refuse war, you should refuse quarrel.

11. **Kungo si men no, nya y'a lon ne** - What the head can carry, the eyes know.

12. **Kunu-kantala, a buka a ya je** - The bird watcher does not look close to home.

13. **Kunku muta n da la, aning doku la mang killing** - To talk about making a farm, and doing the work is not the same.

14. **Wulo meng ka mo ngon-ngong, a buka mo king, bari wulo meng lafita i king na, a ka tambi i noma, f'a si i king** - A dog which barks at people, does not bite, but the dog that wants to bite you, goes round behind you to bite you.

15. **Mem be larango to, wo le ye dabolu long je** - Whoever is on the bed, knows the bedbugs there.

16. **Kuta fula wo le ye nyo king dula long** - The two tortoises know where to bite one.

17. **I nenemang yeo so, I be jio le folo so la** - Before you pierce the fish, you must pierce the water first.

18. **Fankanta mang jauwiya** - Self-protection (foresight) is not bad.

19. **Bi namunang folo, kunung ne folota** - Before today happened, yesterday happened.

20. **I si sateo long nya-o-nya, sate dingo le y'a long ite ti** - However well you know a village, one born there knows it better than you.

21. **Talibo mang fode kuwo long, bari fodeo ye talibe kuwo long** - A pupil does not know what the teacher does, but a teacher knows what the student does.

22. **Tonya buka teriya tinya** - The truth does not spoil friendship.

23. **Bulu kono kunu kilingo, ate le fisayata jamfajang kunu tango ti** - A single bird in the hand, that is better than ten birds far off.

24. **Kuro ke ning tilo be boring** - Do your washing while the sun is out.

25. **Londo soto mu nafulo le ti, londi soto-baliya mu koro le ti. Bari londi-barakantango fanang mulung ne ko montoro buluntango** - Obtaining knowledge is a benefit, lack of knowledge is a trouble. But knowledge which is not blessed is like a watch without hands.

GHANAIAN PROVERBS

Country: Ghana

Capital City: Accra

Area of Country: 238,533km²

Population: 34,258,110

Demonym: Ghanaian

Currency: Ghanaian Cedi (GHS)

Independence Day: 6th March 1957

Official Language: English

National Languages: Ewe, Asante Twi, Akuapem Twi, Fante, Ga, Hausa, Dagaare, Dagbanli, Nzema, Gonja

Other Languages Include: Kasem, Adangme

National Motto: Freedom and Justice

ABOUT EWE

Ewe, also known as Eʋegbe, is spoken in the Volta Region of Ghana, especially in the southern parts bordering Togo. The Ewe ethnic group is one of the major ethnic groups in Ghana, and they have a rich cultural heritage.

EWE – ENGLISH

1. **Wometsoa anyidzefe kowoa anyimlofe o** – Do not take the place where you have fallen as your final resting place.

2. **Wome nyana ame fe avofodiwo le dutofo o** – Do not wash your dirty clothes in public.

3. **Vivo nyowu ko** – A bad child is better than barrenness.

4. **Vi kple no metsona gbedeka o** - A child and the mother do not start the same day.

5. **Tovi be zado, gake nodzido / novi be zamedo o** - Your stepbrother says it is getting too late, but your own brother says it is not too late.

6. **Sabala le nogoo ha, mo le eme** - The onion is round, but there are paths in it.

7. **Nunyala medzea anyi le ko deka dzi zi eve o** - A wise person does not fall on the same hill twice.

8. **Wome noa tome no Lo fe nu dzum o** – You do not stay in a river and then continue abusing the mouth of the crocodile.

9. **Xli gidii mewua ablometi o** - A lot of shouting does not kill the big tree in a public place.

10. **Nunyanya kolikoli, de woxloanu mugamuga** - A person who shows too much knowledge often makes a bad adviser.

11. **No amegbo medzea amenu o** - The thing/person that is with you is never appreciated.

12. **Ne Da du ame kpola de wovona na Vokli** - If a snake has bitten you before, you should be afraid of even an earthworm.

13. **Menye vovo na kutae wogbea alo dona o** - It is not because of fear of death, that you stop sleeping.

14. **Modidi megbona du nuti yina o** - A long journey will not go beyond its destination town.

15. **Dzigbodi wotsona dea afokpa le Fia fe afo** - It is with patience that one removes the sandals from a chief.

16. **De tsitsime aha nona** - The older palm trees produce more wine.

17. **Avu dufu medua ga o** - A dog that chews bones does not chew a piece of metal.

18. **Asideka melea todzo o** - One hand cannot catch a buffalo.

19. **Abo mekpe na wu ata o** - The arm is not bigger than the tie.

20. **Agbebadaa metia agbeto o** - A bad life does not overwhelm the person who leads it.

21. **Amenutoe nyaa efe avovuvu tata** - It is only the owner who knows how to use his tattered clothes.

22. **Avulenu melea Dzata o** - A good hunting dog cannot hunt down a lion.

23. **Dekanyonyo alo manyomanyo ha kpea nu** - Beauty or ugliness can also be shameful.

24. **Koklo be dzianidziani tae ye bobona hafi doa xo** - The chicken says that it is because of humility that it bows down before entering its coop.

25. **Devi masetonu anokae kua to ne** - A child who does not listen to advice, has his ear grabbed by the thorn bush.

GUINEAN PROVERBS

Country: Guinea

Capital City: Conakry

Area of Country: 245,857km ^{2}

Population: 14,260,766

Demonym: Guinean

Currency: Guinea Franc (GNF)

Independence Day: 2nd October 1958

Official Language: French

Other Languages Include: Susu, Pular, Mandinka, Landomba, Kissi, Temne, Limba, Kpelle

National Motto: Work, Justice, Solidarity

ABOUT SUSU

Susu, also known as Sosoxui or Soussou, is a Mande language spoken by the Susu people in several West African countries, primarily in Guinea and Sierra Leone. It is part of the larger Niger-Congo language family.

SUSU – ENGLISH

1. **Allah nan bouboudi khoungni peignema** – It is God who combs the monkey's hair.

2. **Mikhi keren mou noma fera** – Alone we can do nothing.

3. **To koule kore tina a bokhi** - Today the monkey is upstairs, tomorrow he is downstairs.

4. **Ha i mou mikhi kolon, a falaabe n'tara** - If you do not know someone, call their big brother.

5. **Khali Yoube sanyi guirakhi, fo a siga soube fakhade** – Even with a broken foot, the vulture will still go to the slaughterhouse.

6. **Bourokhe mou takhou'ma sii'ra** - The grass does not confide in the goat.

7. **Wouri bou yema kiyoki, a mou findima sogne ra** - Whatever the length of the wood in the river, it will never become a caiman.

8. **Khourou Khourou nan sia n'ga ra fourou** – It is little by little that the mother of many became pregnant.

ABOUT PULAR

Pular is spoken in Guinea, primarily by the Fula people who are one of the major ethnic groups in the country. Fula is spoken in various regions of Guinea, including Fouta Djallon, Upper Guinea, and Forest Guinea.

PULAR – ENGLISH

9. **Mo a'gnima, inai guitema d'en no loubi** - Who hates you, can (even) say that your eyes smell bad.

10. **Sa inni a'moroto goreye joma mwori, khara won fotota soukoundou, kharaye ko ta'jou soukoundou toun woni ton** – If you say you want the same braids and you do not have the same hair, there will only be hair loss.

11. **So a nehi gorko a nehi neɗɗo, so a nehii debbo a nehii ɓesnngu** – If you educate a man, you have educated a person. If you educate a woman, you have educated a family.

12. **Suka ɓuri mowɗo yaawde kono mowɗo ɓuri anndude laawool** – The child walks fast, but it is the old man who knows the way.

13. **Yimɓe ɓurɓe weltaade wona joguuɓe kala ko moyi kono ko moyinooɓe kala ko njogi** — The happiest people are not those who own all the good but are those who do good with what they have.

14. **So neɗɗo moyyi e ma moyyu e num kono so neɗɗo bone e ma hoto bone e mum sibu ɓakkere lawyata ɓakkere** — If a person does you good, repay them good, but if a person does you bad, do not repay them with bad because you do not mud them with mud.

15. **Ko ma ɓundu hora nde ngannden nafoore ndiyam** - We only know the value of water once the well is dry.

16. **Hade ma waylude mbadi ma ngam welde woɓɓe mijo yidirɓema mbaadima ndi** - Before you want to change for others, first think of those who love you as you are.

17. **Mo yiɗi wadde hunnde dañate no waɗiri mo yiɗa wadde dañate ken haɗaɗum wadde** — Who wants to do it finds a solution but who does not want to do it finds an excuse.

18. **Diisi Alla, diisi puddi naage, diisi hirnaange, diisi nano, diisi naamo. Mo adoraali inde Alla o sakkitoray inde Alla** — In the name of God to whom I am refer, in the name of the east and the west, in the name of the north and the south! Whoever does not become accustomed to God at the beginning, will trust him in the end.

19. **Ñagaade yaafuya ne yooɗi kono waasde toñeende ɓuri yoode** — It is good to ask for forgiveness, but even better not to hurt people.

20. **So a yehi ane gooto ma yaaw yettade kono so a yaade woɓɓe ma ya to woɗɗi** — If you leave alone you leave quickly, but if you leave with people, you will reach far.

21. **Mo momti juumre mum hanki momta pinal mum hande** – He who erases his mistakes of yesterday will also erase the lessons learned today.

22. **So jiiduɓe kaɓi ha mbaro ndiri ma arane rone ngalu bammaɓe** – If two brothers fight to the death, a stranger will inherit the property of their father.

MANDINKA – ENGLISH

23. **Lon jan gnakha han, kono lon sebalite** - No matter how long, what happens will happen.

24. **I koun'te taro, i gni wagnaki** – You do not have your head in fire, but your teeth are closed.

25. **Kouloun ba fo *chiiiiii*, a bara se kignema** – If the canoe goes *chiiiiii*, it is because it has reached the sand.

IVORIAN PROVERBS

Country: Ivory Coast
Capital City: Yamoussoukro
Area of Country: 322,462km ^{2}
Population: 14,263,771
Demonym: Ivorian
Currency: West African Franc (XOF)
Independence Day: 7ᵗʰ August 1960
Official Language: French
National Languages Include: Baoulé, Lobi, Mahou, Moore, Dyula, Agni, Guro
National Motto: Union, Discipline, Work

ABOUT BOULÉ

The Baoulé language, also spelled as Baulé or Baule, is a Kwa language spoken by the Baoulé people in Ivory Coast, primarily in the central and eastern regions of the country.

BAOULÉ – ENGLISH

1. **Kɛ be ɲinma'n bo nzue gua, be bue'n diman aklunjuɛ** - When the eye cries, the nose does not rejoice.

2. **Be sá n'ma gba sɛman** - The fingers do not have the same length.

3. **Kɛ nzue tɔ yɛ klɛ be kpan ɔn** - Toads only croak when it rains.

4. **Nzue glɛ kaciman'n sua'n i wafa ng'ɔ ti** - Hot water does not break the house.

5. **Sε a siman klɔ lɔ'n,a ja bae fuε bla** - If you don't know the village, you marry the witch there.

6. **Sran kpεnngbεn nuan nun bɔn, sanguε fíεn kan'n sa numan ndε ng'ɔ kan i sin'n** - The old man's mouth smells bad, but his words have no smell.

7. **Kwlaa naan wá se kε sran kun ti kan'n, dummua nian ɔ bɔbɔ ɔ sran waka** - Before you say someone is thin, you must first look at your own form.

8. **Be awlεn'n m'ɔ be tra yε ɔ kla yo man be gnan like kpa ɔ -** Patience is a golden path.

9. **Kε be ti wo lε, be ja kpɔlε wlaman klé** - When the head is there, the knee does not wear the hat.

10. **Sε sika ti klaman sε o, kaci ɔ pɔsu i Kannga titi** - Despite the beauty of money, remain a slave to your pocket.

11. **Sran nga srε kunmεn i'n n ɔ ti a yakpafuε** - He who is not afraid has no courage.

12. **Kε sa wa ɲán w'ɔ,fɔkɔ bɔbɔ kla yé wɔ like yaya** - When misfortune should befall you, even a cotton pad can hurt you.

13. **Koko'n numan mmua** - Nearby is not far away.

14. **Kε mεn'n yo pɔpɔ'n, sran'm bé káci kplɔ wá fuε** - When life becomes easy, men become lazy.

15. **Sran'm be kloman sran sanguε be be klo sran be sika** - People don't like people but they like people's money.

16. **Be faman be sa bε kleman be klɔ** - You do not show your village with your left hand.

17. **Nanwlε blo be ɲinma'n sanguε ɔ bobo mεn i** - The truth reddens the eyes but does not break them.

18. **Ɔ ti su kɛ ɔ ko yo naan aɲrunɲan'n suman be nga be fali be blɛ ngba kunndɛli i be ndia'n nun lɔ'n ɔ timan bɔbɔ sangue ɔ b'a wá trán sran ng'ɔ fufuli kunndɛli i ndia'n su** - Glory rarely accompanies the memory of those who have used their lives to seek it, but it comes to sit on the modest grave of those who searched for it.

19. **Anuman nin waka be tuman ngondin, afin kɛ wlan lelele ɔ ko tran su ekun** - The bird never talks with the tree because it always ends up landing there.

20. **Sɛ wa kuman jrá a klwa ɲɛnmɛn i kplo** - You cannot get a lion's skin without killing it.

21. **Yɛbuɛ nga be fá y'a yɛ be to'n i kpɛ sunman lika ɔ ɲan man anuman ga be sunnzun nin Kɛ be kun i** - The pebble of anger rarely kills the targeted bird.

22. **Sɛ ɔ wun fu a fá atin kun ngbɛn sa,ɛ ko fite klɔ kun su mɔ ɔ yo w'ɔ nsisɔ ɔ** - If you take the path of I do not care you, will end up in the village of if I knew.

23. **Sɛ wá nán kpɛnman nzue ba, nán srí sran nga nzue nin di i** - When you have not yet crossed the river, do not mock the one who drowns.

24. **Boli nga wá wun ɔ sroman laliɛ ba** — A dead goat is not afraid of a knife.

25. **Talɛ i ja wun yɛ be wun sran ng'ɔ si sua kplan niɔn** - It is at the foot of the wall that we see the real mason.

KENYAN PROVERBS

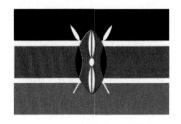

Country: Kenya

Capital City: Nairobi

Area of Country: 582,646km ^{2}

Population: 55,341,145

Demonym: Kenyan

Currency: Kenyan Shilling (KES)

Independence Day: 12th December 1963

Official Language: Swahili, English

National Language: Swahili

Other Languages Include: Maasai, Oromo, Kikuyu, Kuria, Samia, Gusii

National Motto: All pull together.

ABOUT SWAHILI

Swahili, also known as Kiswahili, is a Bantu language spoken by millions of people in East Africa and parts of Central Africa. It is one of the official languages of several East African countries and is used as a lingua franca in the region. Swahili is primarily spoken in the East African countries of Kenya, Tanzania, Uganda, Rwanda, Burundi, and parts of Somalia, the Democratic Republic of Congo and South Sudan. It has also influenced languages and cultures in neighbouring regions.

SWAHILI - ENGLISH

1. **Maisha ina mizimu** - Life has seasons.

2. **Afadhali kuwa maskini na uishi sana badala ya kuwa tajiri na ufe ukiwa kijana** - It is better to be poor and live long than rich and die young.

3. **Jicho la Mungu huona kwa upana** - The eye of God is large.

4. **Jicho lililo tembea ndilo elevu** - Clever is the eye that has travelled.

5. **Ndovu anaweza angushwa na mumea anayetambaa** - The elephant can be tripped by a creeping plant.

6. **Mtoto anaweza ona wezi kabla ya babake** - The child may see thieves before the father does.

7. **Mtaa usio zungumziwa hauwezi kujengwa** - The village which is not discussed is not built.

8. **Wakati mti uliyokauka una anguka, una haribu mti uliyo na nguvu** - The withered tree will destroy the healthy tree when it falls.

9. **Watu huwa wajinga mwanzo lakini huerevuka kwa mazoea** - We begin by being foolish and we become wise by experience.

10. **Fahamu kile unaona kama vile unafahamu mahali unapoishi** - Be as familiar with observation as you are with the place you live.

11. **Hata jambo/kitu/mtu nayedharauliwa anaweza faulu** - Even that which is despised can triumph.

12. **Hakuna anayeweza sema atakaa mahali fulani milele, ni milima tu isiyo hama** - Nobody can say he is settled anywhere forever; it is only the mountains which do not move from their places.

13. **Kichwa kimoja haiwezi tumia maarifa yote** - One head cannot consume all knowledge.

14. **Si kupata ambayo ni shinda, shinda ni kuweka ulichopata** - It is not acquisition that is difficult, it is retention.

15. **Mambo ya Mungu haiwezi kuvurutwa kwa mkono** - That which is Godly cannot be pushed away with the forearm.

16. **Usitengeneze ukuta wa mtu mwingine hadi umeona ukuta wako** - Do not repair another man's fence until you have seen your own.

17. **Watoto ni mwezi ulio angaza** - The children are the bright moon.

18. **Hauwezi fanya maji ipande mlima** - You cannot force water up a hill.

19. **Mtu hushindwa na hadaa zake/kundanganya kwake** - Man is always beaten by his own tricks.

20. **Usionyeshe mwewe jinsi itapaa kwa hewa** - Do not show the hawk how to fly.

21. **Mtaka cha uvunguni sharti ainame** — One who wants to get something under the bed must bend.

22. **Usemi wa wazee umebarikiwa** - The words of the elders are blessed.

23. **Punda milia hupeleka milia yake popote aendapo** - A zebra takes its stripes wherever it goes.

24. **Wazo mpya hufuata wazo mzee** - A new idea follows an old one.

25. **Shingo haliwezi kuwa kichwa** - The neck cannot become the head.

LIBERIAN
PROVERBS

Country: Liberia

Capital City: Monrovia

Area of Country: 111,369km ^{2}

Population: 5,444,364

Demonym: Liberian

Currency: Liberian Dollar (LRD)

Independence Day: 26th July 1847

Official Language: English

Other Languages Include: Bassa, Grebo, Dan, Mano, Loma

National Motto: The love of liberty bought us here.

ABOUT BASSA

Bassa, also known as Bassa-Kpelle, is a Kru language spoken by the Bassa people in Liberia, Sierra Leone, and other parts of West Africa. It is one of the Niger-Congo languages.

BASSA – ENGLISH

1. **Nyon-vehnnehn se vonon behin, keh oh dyuo gbaa ka** - The elder is unable to fight, but he has a rich experience of struggles.

2. **So-gehn ni cheh-eh oh deh wa** – A chicken egg cannot turn its hen over.

3. **Ni da wouun hwedein ni, oh nyu tonon** - Water becomes saliva when it remains in the mouth too long.

4. **Nyon ni po gaa-kon** - There is no need to augment a man.

5. **Dech poein-dyi hweh ke wa kidi tede** - Red ants bend a nest only when they are united.

6. **Son dyoa do ni fia gbinnin** - A single hand cannot coil a boa constrictor.

7. **M pinin m mion-kpo kopo mu ni, wa zain m se pinin dyede** - If you cook yourself in a tin can, people will dish you up with a piece of bamboo stick.

8. **Behin-behin di pooh-whehn** - Only peers eat roasted palm nuts together.

9. **M dyi koch chehn-ehn dyuo ni, m dieh piuu** - If you know how to butcher an ant, you will eat its liver.

10. **Duun-ku-nyon ni se de** - No diligent person can remain in poverty.

11. **Pee-nyuehn ni se hwio xwadaun** - Night must come to end the pleasures of the day.

12. **Nyon se-dyuo ke zon-zon** - The day dawns when one is unaware of it.

13. **Nyon-vehnnehn mon mu-dedein bohke. Oh ku dyoh-hwodo** - An elder is a bath-tub; it restrains laughter.

14. **Nyon ni di nyon mue-do bii dehin-deh** - One cannot eat a delicious meal for another.

15. **Wodo-wodo mon ni dukpa, oh ni so-pehn-nain** - A blood relation is a river gulf of ages; it is unmovable by anything.

16. **Niehn dehbeh nyon mueh, pa nyon bidi tehbeh mu** - Water enters your bottle when it loves you.

17. **M dehbeh-ch baun-baun muin, m behdeheh sein mu** — By being greedy for more, you can miss everything.

18. **Kpe-ji ni vonin gannan** - A leopard of authority never fights by strength.

19. **Banan se-muge** - Wealth is not discriminatory.

20. **Hwidii-de-gbea ni kpa kaunka** - A hopeful crab basket can fail to catch the intended crab.

21. **Gedepooh faa dyuch wonon bedech mu po-deh** - The God who split his child's mouth, has something to put in it.

22. **Wudu se widi** - Words are not money to be spent.

23. **Dyi-kan-naan dee ke oh zi banan-dyi** - To be healthy is sweeter than being rich.

24. **Gedepooh ni zi-kpodo** - God never passes on the side of injustice.

25. **Jaa se behn-indeh bun-wehnin** – The truth does not need any decoration.

LIBYAN PROVERBS

Country: Libya
Capital City: Tripoli
Area of Country: 1,759,540km ^{2}
Population: 6,905,270
Demonym: Libyan
Currency: Libyan Dinar (LYD)
Independence Day: 24th December 1951
Official Language: Arabic
Other Languages Include: Libyan Arabic, Tedaga, Nafusi, Suknah

ABOUT ARABIC

Arabic is a Semitic language spoken by millions of people. About 42% of Arabic speakers live on the continent of Africa and about 150 million Africans speak some form of Arabic as a first language. A further 50 to110 million are estimated to speak it as a second language.

ARABIC – ENGLISH

1. وَجَّد الخُطَب قبل النار - You must prepare the wood before making a fire.

2. التعلم زينه يف الرخاء ، ملاذ يف المحنة و رخدم يف الشيخوخة - Learning is an ornament in prosperity, a refuge in adversity and a provision in old age.

3. الشرّ يعمي العينين – Hunger blinds the eyes.

4. البشر ليسوا ةكئلام - Men are not angels.

5. ىسني الألم ثيد الربح - Pain is forgotten when gain follows.

6. دماغ الفرطاس قريب لربّي - The bald man's skull is close to Heaven.

7. الشبعة تعمل بدعة – Opulence leads to fantasy.

8. ألّي فيه طبيعة ما ينساها غيرَ مات وخلاها – He who has a habit will only be able to abandon it once covered with a shroud.

9. المال معذ الخادم و سئد السيد - Money is good servant but a bad master.

10. بحدي لا ما عمسيد بحدي ما لقيد نه - He who says what he likes shall hear what he does not like.

11. يمشو الرجلين لوين يحبّو الخواطر – The feet move towards where the owner wants them to go.

12. الظلم يذهب بعقول العقلاء - Oppression makes a wise man mad.

13. عينك هي ميزانك – Your eye is your scale.

14. الدَّيْن شَرُ أَنْواع الفَقْر - It is worse to be in debt than to be poor.

15. مَن طَلَبَ أخًا بلا عَيْب بقِيَ بلا أخ - He who seeks a friend without fault remains without a friend.

16. لا تسألوا نعء أشياء إن تبدو مكد مكئوسة - Never trouble trouble until trouble troubles you. It only doubles trouble and troubles others too.

17. الأعور بين العميان ملك - In the kingdom of the blind, the one-eyed are kings.

18. رُبّ أخ لم تلده أمَك – A good friendship is a second relationship.

19. اللسان الصامت عنصيد الرجال – A still tongue makes a wise head.

20. أضحك كحضيد كد العالم ، و ابك كبد وحيدا - Laugh and the world laughs with you, weep and you weep alone.

21. لا نكد دبع هواك - Master your temper lest it masters you.

22. من جعل نفسه نعجة أكلته الذئاب - He that makes himself a sheep, shall be eaten by the wolf.

23. لا تلقوا بأيديكم إلى التهلكة - Do not put your head in the lion's mouth.

24. العاقل من اعتبر بغيره - Learn wisdom by the follies of others.

25. نقاء الإنسان فرصة لاقترابه من الله - Man's extremity is God's opportunity.

MALAGASY PROVERBS

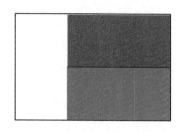

Country: Madagascar
Capital City: Antananarivo
Area of Country: 586,884km²
Population: 30,489,280
Demonym: Malagasy
Currency: Malagasy Ariary (MGA)
Independence Day: 26ᵗʰ June 1960
Official Languages: Malagasy, French
National Motto: Love, Ancestral-land, Progress

ABOUT MALAGASY

Malagasy is the language spoken in Madagascar. It is classified as an Austronesian language, specifically belonging to the Malayo-Polynesian subgroup. Malagasy is one of the few Austronesian languages spoken outside of Southeast Asia and the Pacific and has incorporated loanwords from African, Arabic, French, and other languages.

MALAGASY – ENGLISH

1. **Aleo meloka amin'ny olombelona to izay meloka amin'ny Andriamanitra** - Better to be guilty towards men than to be guilty towards God.

2. **Manao an'Andriamanitra tsy hisy, ka mitsambiky mikimpy** - To deny the existence of God is to jump with your eyes closed.

3. **Aleo ratsy tarehy ka tsara fanahy, to isay tsara tarehy ka ratsy fanahy** - It is better to be ugly and good, than to be handsome and mean.

4. **Ny olombelona tsy fo vato, fa fo emboka** - The heart of man is not made of stone but of resin.

5. **Aza manao so tapany** — Do not do good by halves.

6. **Mita be tsy lanin'ny mamba** - When there are many to cross the river, we are not devoured by caimans

7. **Manaova soa ampiantany, fa misy hiankina, ary manaova soa vato, fa misy hipetrahana** - Do good to a wall and you can lean on it; Do good to a stone and you can sit on it.

8. **Ady amin'ny adala, ka ny hendry no miala** - In an argument with a fool, it is the sensible man who withdraws.

9. **Izay be ditra be nenina** - A lot of stubbornness, a lot of regrets.

10. **Aza manao kamo fa tenda** - Do not be lazy while being greedy.

11. **Avo fijery ny Andriamanitra ka mahita ny takona** - God looking down sees what is hidden.

12. **Ataovy fitia lamban'akoho ka faty no hisarahana** - In love, be like the hen and her plumage, only death separates them.

13. **Manao rafimaroroka, ka malaky mirodona** - Construction done too quickly will collapse in a short time.

14. **Maizina ny andro, azo tsilovina, lalina ny rano, azo lakanina, lalina ny hady, azo toharina; fa ni ratsy tsy mba azon-kevitra** - If it is dark, one can lighten, if the water is deep, one can cross it by canoe, if the ditch is deep, one can descend by a ladder, but a bad action is without remedy.

15. **Ny teny malemy mahamora harena** - Kind words facilitate the acquisition of wealth.

16. **Ny olombelona tsy miditra am-pitarihan-tokana** - Not all men follow the same path.

17. **Ny vola toy ny vahiny, tonga anio, lasa rahampitso** - Money is like a stranger, it arrives today, and it will leave tomorrow.

18. **Ratsy tokoa ny lainga, fa ny mpandainga aza tsy tia azy** - Lying is very bad, because the liar himself does not like it.

19. **Aza ny hafohezan'ny andro no alaina, fa nu halavan'ny taona heverina** - Do not consider the brevity of the days but think of the length of the years.

20. **Aza manirina olon-tsy afaka aina** — Do not close the eyes of someone who has not died yet.

21. **Raha tsy mahala izay teny tsy mety, tsy mba lehilahy** - You are not a man if you do not know how to say no to a bad word.

22. **Ny manenjika ny osa enjenhin'ny mahery kosa** - Those who pursue or persecute the weak, will in turn be pursued or persecuted by the strong.

23. **Ny fihavanana tahaka ny volon-kotona: hatonina, manalavitra; halavirina, manatona** - Friendship is like seaweed: when you get closer, they move away, and when you move away, they come closer.

24. **Ny nenina tsy eo aloha hananatra fa aoriana handatsa** - Regret does not arrive before to warn you, but afterwards to taunt you.

25. **Ny valala tsy indroa mandry am-bavahady** - The grasshopper won't come and knock on your door twice.

MALAWIAN PROVERBS

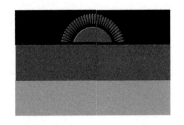

Country: Malawi Capital City: Lilongwe

Area of Country: 118,480km^2

Population: 21,054,803

Demonym: Malawian

Currency: Malawian Kwacha (MWK)

Independence Day: 6th July 1964

Official Languages: English

Other Languages Include: Chewa (Nyanja), Yao, Lomwe, Ngonde, Lambya

National Motto: Unity and Freedom

ABOUT CHEWA (NYANJA)

Chewa, also known as Nyanja, is a Bantu language spoken by the Chewa people. It is primarily spoken in Malawi but is also spoken in countries such as Zambia, Mozambique, and Zimbabwe.

CHEWA (NYANJA) – ENGLISH

1. **Mau a akulu-akulu akoma akagonera** – The words of the elders become sweet the day after.

2. **Iri ndi mace sikugwa m'mbuna** – Who keeps close to his mother does not fall in the trap.

3. **Samva mnzako ndi tsiru** – He who does not listen to his neighbour is a fool.

4. **Tsamba likagwa manyazi agwira mtengo** – When a leaf falls down the shame will be on the tree.

5. **Anafa kalikongwe nzeru ya yekha** – The squirrel who trusted in its own wisdom fell to its death.

6. **Mnyanga sulemera mwini** – The tusks are never too heavy for the owner.

7. **Ciswe cimodzi siciumba culu** – One white ant does not build an anthill.

8. **Kupatsa nkuika** – To give is to put aside.

9. **Mnzako akapsa ndebvu mzimire** – When your friend's beard catches fire, extinguish it for him.

10. **Odwala agawa m'phika** – Even the one who is sick shares what is in the cooking pot.

11. **Pepani sapoletsa cilonda** – Saying sorry does not heal a wound.

12. **Phwiti akahuta salawira mtondo** – When the sparrow is satisfied, it does not bid farewell to the pounding mortar.

13. **Usamati 'ndathawa mlomo' uli ponse ponse** – Never say "I am running away from gossip", for gossip is everywhere.

14. **Ukasauka usamagwira nyanga** – When you are poor do not take hold of the horn.

15. **Wobvala nyanda salumpha moto** - He who wears bark-cloth should not jump over fire.

16. **Manong'onong'o anapha ubwenzi** – Back-biting killed friendship.

17. **'Uli dere' nkulinga utayenda naye** – You can say "He is like this" only when you have walked with him.

18. **Ukakhala wopanda cala usamadana nkuloza** – When you have no finger do not dislike pointing.

19. **Cikomekome cankhuyu mkati muli nyerere** – From the outside the fig looks very appealing, but inside it is full of ants.

20. **Cibwenzi ca nkhwangwa cokoma pokwera** – The friendship of an axe is sweet only when climbing.

21. **Tsabola wakale sawawa** – Old pepper is no longer hot.

22. **Mutu ukakula sulewa nkhonya** – When the head is big it cannot avoid punches.

23. **Citsiru cidaona nkhondo** – It was the fool who saw the enemy approaching.

24. **Mtaya makoko saiwala; aiwala ndi mdya nyemba** – One who throws away bean-pods never forgets; one who eats the beans does forget.

25. **Kanthu ndi khama** – Success presupposes effort.

MALIAN PROVERBS

Country: Mali
Capital City: Bamako
Area of Country: 1,241,238km²
Population: 23,457,596
Demonym: Malian
Currency: West African Franc (XOF)
Independence Day: 22nd September 1960
Official Languages: Bambara, Hassaniya Arabic, Bozo, Arabic, Minyanka, Dogon, Tamasheq, Songhay, Maninke, Kassonke, Fula, Bobo, Soninke, Senufo
National Motto: One people, one goal, one faith.

ABOUT BAMBARA

Bambara, also known as Bamanankan, is a Mande language spoken primarily by the Bambara people in Mali. It is one of the major languages in Mali and is used in various aspects of daily life, culture, and communication.

BAMBARA – ENGLISH

1. **Ala tɛ juru di an ma nka a bɛ an ka juru le sara** - God does not lend to us but he pays our debts.

2. **Ni sisi man di i ye i tɛ se fana ka sarabɔn sɔrɔ** - He who cannot stand smoke does not get coal either.

3. **Nin Ala ye fɛn di i m'an, a t'i fa n'i ba tɔgɔ ɲiniga** - When God gives to you, he does not ask for the names of your father and mother.

4. **Nafolo, lɔniya, famaya jamana tɛ o fɛn saba fɛ** - Fortune, knowledge and power have no homeland.

5. **Duniɲa ɲanfɛyɔrɔ n'a kɔfɛyɔrɔ kaɲi** - The world is both ahead and behind.

6. **An kana kɛ kasaratɔ ye an ka bolodɛn duru kosɔn** - Let us not be victims of our five fingers.

7. **Yiri ma nan boɲen o boɲen jɛnde fitini le b'a la bɛn** - However big the tree, it is the little axe that cuts it down.

8. **Jamana tɛ daamu ni tɔɔrɔ fɛ, o bɛ ta yɔrɔ Min k'u diya** - Happiness and unhappiness have no homeland, they are where God wants them to be.

9. **Sanpɛrɛn tuma na, bɛɛ b'a janto a ka kunkolo la** - Under the storm, everyone takes care of their own heads.

10. **Wuludenin be se bori la nka wuru kɔrɔ bɛ kɔngo dɔ ka tɛmɛ a kan** - The dog of youth runs fast, but the dog of old age knows the forest better than he does.

11. **I bɛ dunan bisimila cogo min na tabali kan, o b' a to u bɛ dumuni kɛ ka ɲɛ walima ka ban domini na** - The way you welcome the guest to the table allows them to eat well or not.

12. **I be tagama ni fɛn jugu kɔnɔtɔ minw ye, n'a sɔrɔ i bena kelɛn ta** - Of the nine vices you frequent, you risk adopting one.

13. **Misimuso b'a dɛn ɲɔnti nka a t'a kɔniya** - The cow pushes her calf but does not hate it.

14. **Ka kan ni fɛn dɔ ye ani kunandiya tɛ kelɛn ye** - Having merit and being lucky are two.

15. **Sagoya bɛ dɛmɛ barikaman lase min be bara kɛ n'a ye** - Willpower powerfully helps whoever uses it.

16. **Ɲɛnamaya ye dɔn dé ye, o ye a dɔnkɛ siɲɛ kélén dɔrɔn** - Life is a ballet, you only dance it once.

17. **Koo bɛɛ ni a sababu** - Every event has its cause.

18. **Tile m'a kan ka bin siɲɛ fla baara kelɛn kan** - The sun should not set twice on the same work.

19. **Min bɛ ɲanagali kɛ a tɛ fili** - The one who asks is not likely to make a mistake.

20. **Kɛnɛya ka fisa ka tɛmɛ cɛɲi kan** - Good health is better than beauty.

21. **N'an be caaman sɔrɔ, an makoyafɛnw be caya fana** - The more we receive, the more we ask.

22. **Kansi tɛ hadamaden na, a minɛni ye a da kuma ye** - Man has no mane, his grip is the words of his mouth.

23. **Dɛn ye mɔkɔrɔba ka tintinbere** - The child is the stick of old age.

24. **Ka sinɔgɔ kongo la can kama o ka fisa ka tɛmɛ ta ngalon tigɛ ani ka da kɔnɔ fani na** - Telling the truth and going to bed hungry is better than lying and going to bed hungry.

25. **Min sɔna juru la, a sɔna fana kɛlɛ la** - He who accepts credit accepts quarrel.

MAURITANIAN PROVERBS

Country: Mauritania

Capital City: Nouakchott

Area of Country: 1,030,000m²

Population: 4,893,455

Demonym: Mauritanian

Currency: Mauritanian Ouguiya (MRU)

Independence Day: 28ᵗʰ November 1960

Official Language: Arabic

Other Languages Include: Hassaniya Arabic, French, Wolof, Soninke, Berber

National Motto: Honour, Fraternity, Justice

ABOUT HASSANIYA ARABIC

Hassaniya Arabic, also known as Hassani or Hassaniyya is widely spoken throughout Mauritania. It is the mother tongue of the Maure (or Moors) ethnic group, which constitutes a significant portion of the Mauritanian population. Hassaniya is spoken in several countries in North and West Africa including Mali, Western Sahara, Algeria, Morocco, and parts of Niger and Libya.

HASSANIYA ARABIC – ENGLISH

1. باش تعرف شي اراصك شغل أدماغك، باش تعاون الناس أتعاطف أمعاهم – To manage yourself, use your head; to manage others, use your heart.

2. باش أكبار أراص، باش أكبارت الجمجمة - The bigger the head, the bigger the headaches.

97

3. ‏أل يبق الفظ يشتقل ألها‏ - He who loves money must labour.

4. ‏إلى أنكب الماء، ما معناه عن لگدح مدگدگ‏ - It is only the water that is spilt; the calabash is not broken.

5. ‏رگاج أشبه يصنت أكثر ويتكلم أشوي‏ - One must talk little and listen much.

6. ‏الغبي أجمل من معرظ‏ – A fool is more ignorant than a stone.

7. ‏أطش نى تكبار تعود اتقصص‏ – Too large a morsel chokes the child.

8. ‏أل بين الحگ والكذب، گد عرظ أربع أصابع‏ – Between truth and lies, there is just the width of four fingers.

9. ‏"ياسر من الصحبة إگد إعدلك إتندم‏ – Too many friends can become a source of remorse.

10. ‏الدنيا ألا فترة زمنية وتوف.‏ – Life is an inescapable timeline.

11. ‏اشخص الغبي هو ال مايخرص البعيد، اراع الى فذل گدام عينيه‏ – A simpleton can see no further than the end of his nose.

12. ‏الكلمة المؤذية أمظ من الموس، جرح الموس يبر يغير جرح الكلمة مايبرة‏ – A cutting word is worse than a bowstring; a cut may heal but the cut of the tongue does not.

13. ‏ماخالگ حد أغبى من الشخص أل متكاسل ومع ذكامل يشكي من ذاك ال رادل ملان‏ – No one is more foolish than the lazy person who cries for his fate.

14. ‏نى يخبطك لحمار وتگوم تخبط، أنت او لحمار ألا سيان‏ - If a donkey gives you a kick and you kick him back; you both become donkeys.

15. ‏الشيبان لعمى نى يرجعل بصر دور يعرف نعمت لبصر‏ - If an old man regained his vision after being blind, he would know the importance of eyes.

16. ‏الجار قبل الدار‏ – Find out about your neighbours before buying the house.

17. أساس أي صحبة هو الصراحة والإخلاص - The most faithful companions of friendship are frankness and sincerity.

18. البقي هو أزين شي وأمرّ شي في نفس الوقت – Love is the sweetest and most bitter thing.

19. حفظ الموجود أولى من طلب المفقود – A penny in the hand is worth more than a hundred in debt.

20. التعليم في الصغر كالنقش في الحجر – What we learned in our youth is never lost.

21. طلب العلم ماعند حدود – The quest for knowledge has no limits.

22. أل اخرص مرجن ما اشيط اعليه – If you watch your pot, your food will not burn.

23. شوفه عينين ماشافت عين وحدةً – Two eyes see better than one.

24. ماه الا كل نبتة تعطيك الفواكه - Not all the flowers of a tree produce fruit.

25. الحجرة من أيد صاحبك تعود تفاحة – A stone from the hand of a friend is an apple.

MAURITIAN PROVERBS

Country: Mauritius

Capital City: Port Louis

Area of Country: 2,040km ^{2}

Population: 1,300,893

Demonym: Mauritian

Currency: Mauritian Rupees (MUR)

Independence Day: 12th March 1968

Official Languages: English, French

Other Languages Include: Mauritian Creole (Morisien), Bhojpuri, Tamil

National Motto: Star and key of the Indian Ocean.

ABOUT MAURITIAN CREOLE (MORISIEN)

Mauritian Creole, also known as Morisien, is a Creole language spoken in Mauritius. It is the mother tongue of most of the population and serves as a lingua franca for people of various ethnic backgrounds.

MAURITIAN CREOLE (MORISIEN) – ENGLISH

1. **Qa qui ti bien fere, zames ti mal fere** - What is rightly done is never wrongly done.

2. **Bon bagout cappe lavie** - A good gab saves one's life.

3. **Zamais bef senti so corne trop iourd** - The ox never finds his horns too heavy to carry.

4. **Ca qui fine goute larac zames perdi son gout** - He who once tasted arrack never forgets the taste.

5. **Ca qui tine poelon qui cone so prix lagresse** - It is the one who holds the skillet that knows the cost of lard.

6. **Qa qui touye son lecorps travaille pour leveres** - He who kills his own body, works for the worms.

7. **Qaquene senti so doulere** - Everybody has his own troubles.

8. **Azordi casae en fin; dimain tape lansrouti** - Well-dressed today; only a loincloth tomorrow.

9. **Qatte qui fine bourle av dife pere lacende** - When a cat has been once burned by fire, it is afraid of even cinders.

10. **Coment to tale to natte faut to dourmi** - As you spread your mat, so must you lie.

11. **Conseillere napas payere** - The adviser is not the payer.

12. **Coq cante divant la porte, doumounde vini** - When the cock crows before the door, somebody is coming.

13. **Dimounde qui fere larzent, napas larzent qui fere dimounde** - It is the man who makes the money; it is not the money that makes the man.

14. **Faut pas casse so male avant li fine mir** - Do not pluck one's corn before it is ripe.

15. **Gouie passe difil sivre** - Where the needle passes thread will follow.

16. **Larzan napas trouve dans lipied milet** - Money is not to be found in a mule's hoof.

17. **Larzan napas ena famille** - Money has no blood relations.

18. **Lhere lamontagne bourle, tout dimounde cone; Ihere lequere bourle, qui cone?** - When the mountain burns, everybody knows it; when the heart burns, who knows it?

19. **Lizie napas ena balizaze** — The eyes have no boundary.

20. **Maladie vine lahaut ieve; li alle lahaut tourtie** - Sickness comes riding upon a hare; but goes away riding upon a tortoise.

21. **Montagnes zames zoinde, domounde zoinde** - Only mountains never meet, men meet.

22. **Napas remie fimie sec** - Do not stir up dry manure.

23. **Quand diabe alle lamesse li caciette so laquee** - When the devil goes to mass he hides his tail.

24. **Zames disel dire li sale** - The salt never says that it is salty.

25. **Quand prend trop boucoup, li glisse** - Grab too much, and it slips away from you.

MOROCCAN PROVERBS

Country: Morocco

Capital City: Rabat

Area of Country: 710,850km ^{2}

Population: 37,925,082

Demonym: Moroccan

Currency: Moroccan Dirham (MAD)

Independence Day: 18th November 1955

Official Languages: Arabic, Standard Moroccan Amazigh

Other Languages Include: French, Moroccan Arabic, Hassaniya Arabic

National Motto: God, the Country, the King.

ABOUT STANDARD MOROCCON AMAZIGH

Standard Moroccan Amazigh, also known as Standard Moroccan Berber or simply Standard Tamazight, is a standardised form of the Amazigh language used in Morocco. It was granted official status in Morocco's 2011 constitution, recognising it as one of the Morocco's official languages.

STANDARD MOROCCOAN AMAZIGH – ENGLISH

1. **Inna mi trit adṛẓmm tlkmtn s ufus ṛẓmn** – Extend your hand, and doors will open.

2. **Yuf wawal ifulkin urgh** – Beautiful words are better than gold.

3. **Afgan nna ur ittikṣuḍn tidt ur dars ma ittikṣuḍ gh tkerkas** – The man who fears no truth has nothing to fear from lies.

4. **Iɣt ur ilkm umuc ar ittini tjja** – When the cat cannot reach the meat it says that it is rancid.

5. **Nniyt aysserbaḥen** – Good faith brings prosperity.

6. **Amettul nna gh ur tendert, ur rad gi-s temgert** – A field where you do not groan in pain, you will not reap its fruit.

7. **Ur d illi ufus i tnznar mqqar ẓẓant** – The hand must take charge of the nose even if it stinks.

8. **Frḍ i warraw n rnddn mag ttddun winnk** – Sweep the path for the children of others; yours too will walk on it.

9. **Asif ifstan a itsttan** – It is the silent river that engulfs.

10. **Bu yils, midden ak wins** – He with a sweet tongue, owns the world.

11. **Wanna ur imurriyn ar ittɣal izd urarn gan idrarn** – He who has not travelled thinks that hills are mountains.

12. **Iɣ tga tidt tanakkaḍt tikerkas ar nqqan** – If the truth is horrible, lies are murderous.

13. **Aram ura iẓṛa ayiwt-nns** – The camel does not see its hump.

14. **Tayri n tidet tga zun d azɣuɣ gguten willi fellas isawaln macc drusen willi tt iẓṛan** – True love is like ghosts which everybody talks about, and few have seen.

15. **Asqsi lli bahra yxcnn igat walli ur jju tsaqsat** – The worst question is the one never asked.

16. **Aẓawan iga tirmt n tayri** – Let music be the nourishment of love.

17. **Tumla ifulkin tuf ayda iggutn** – A good reputation is better than wealth.

18. **Serkat Niyya** – Have good intentions.

19. **Aẓawan d akniw n tlelli** – Music is synonymous with freedom.

20. **Assn iga tirmt n ungim** – Knowledge is food for the mind.

21. **Aynna-yk imla zzeman ur-a ijellu** – Life's lessons, once learned, are never forgotten.

22. **Ifulki bahra ulili mac iḥra** – Oleander is very beautiful, but it is bitter.

23. **Wanna ygan tahruyt ccant uccann** – He who stutters is eaten by wolves.

24. **Agḍiḍ ɣ ufus yuf sin ɣ iggi n waddag** – A bird in the hand is worth two in the bush.

25. **Kra illan iṭṭaf ixf** – Everything has a beginning.

MOZAMBICAN PROVERBS

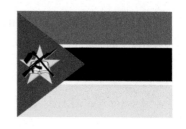

Country: Mozambique

Capital City: Maputo

Area of Country: 799,380km²

Population: 34,115,533

Demonym: Mozambican

Currency: Metical (MZN)

Independence Day: 25th June 1975

Official Language: Portuguese

Other Languages Include: Sena, Tsonga, Lomwe, Changana, Makhuwa

ABOUT SENA

The Sena language, also known as Cisena or Chisena, is a Bantu language spoken by the Sena people in Mozambique. It is one of the many Bantu languages found in Southern Africa. Sena is primarily spoken in the central and northern regions of Mozambique, particularly along the Zambezi River and its surrounding areas. It is one of the major languages in these regions.

SENA - ENGLISH

1. **Kupasa nkhubzala** – To give is to sow.

2. **Ntsambu kulira – nkhukhala ziwiri** – Bangles sound when they are two.

3. **Kumana ndzako nkhudzimana wekha** – To refuse to give to your neighbour is to refuse to be given.

4. **Mmudzi si muako nkhudia na nyalipobsue** – In the house which is not yours you may have to eat with the enemy.

5. **Unganyera dalo mangwana unagona kupi** – If you excrete in the lodging house where shall you sleep tomorrow?

6. **Kubala kwa ndzako nkwako** – Your neighbours childbearing is your own.

7. **Nkulu afunye muendo toera muana apite** – Let the older person move his leg so that the young one may pass.

8. **Ntsima ya m'ndzako hinakalisirwa alendo** – Let the food that belongs to another not make you halt a traveller.

9. **Banja ndi gombe, hinanesa kugomoka taiu** – The family is like a steep riverbank, it crumbles quickly.

10. **Baba ua ndzako ndi ntsengua ia madzi** – The father of your friend is like a basket of water.

11. **Kumanga nyumba pa njira nkhumangira alendo** - To build a house beside the road is to build it for travellers.

12. **Leka kukamulira nkaka pantsi** – Do not squirt milk onto the ground.

13. **Sindi kulira nkhukhala na mphako** – The squirrel squeaks when it has a hole nearby.

14. **Diekera na akulu akulu akudziwe** – Flatter the elders so that you get privileges from them.

15. **Cha mndzako si chako** – What belongs to another is not yours.

16. **Nyanga ya kwenda kutali hinasoa gulai** – Does a stream which travels a long way not meander?

17. **Chidima ndi ambala, unaphata mbava** – Darkness is a brother; in it you can catch a thief.

18. **Nkhuku inakuzua na njala inateia bi** – The unfed hen will not lay eggs.

19. **Mphambvu za ng'ona ziri mu m'chira** – The strength of the crocodile is in its tail.

20. **Ntima ndi muti, panafuna io unanemera** – The heart is free, it grows where it wants.

21. **Mbalame ia ntsetseti inabveka ingalira** – The bird in a forest is heard only when it sings.

22. **Lemelere apita mnyumba mwa sauke: sauke apita mnyumba mwa lemelere** – The rich entered the house of the poor: the poor entered the house of the rich.

23. **Kukomerwa na kokota, nkhupha nyama** – To be satisfied with a fishing net is when you catch fish with it.

24. **Fodia wako ndiye ali pa mphuno** – It is the tobacco that is in your nose that belongs to you.

25. **Soliri kulira nkhukhala na mtendere** – A bird sings when it is in peace.

NAMBIAN PROVERBS

Country: Nambia
Capital City: Windhoek
Area of Country: 824,292km²
Population: 2,614,091
Demonym: Nambian
Currency: Nambian Dollar (NAD)
Independence Day: 21ˢᵗ March 1990
Official Language: English
Other Languages Include: Oshiwambo (Oshikwanyama Dialect,
Oshindonga Dialect), Khoekhoegowab, Afrikaans, Otjiherero,
RuKwangali
National Motto: Unity, Liberty, Justice

ABOUT OSHIWAMBO (OSHIKWANYAMA DIALECT)

Oshiwambo is a Bantu language spoken in Namibia, primarily in the northern regions of the country. It is one of the most widely spoken languages in Namibia and holds cultural and linguistic significance for the Ovambo people, who make up the largest ethnic group in Namibia. Within Oshiwambo, there are several dialects and Oshikwanyama is one of the prominent ones.

OSHIWAMBO (OSHIKWANYAMA DIALECT – ENGLISH)

1. **Okapundi kashona ke dule omutyonghe** – Having something is better than nothing.

2. **She ku pe Pamba tambula, Shekupe Kalunga Kanangobe Shambekela nomaoko avali** – One must accept everything that God is giving him.

3. **Limbandungila onhapo yamukweni hayo yoye** – Run at your own pace as you cannot compare yourself with someone else's pace.

4. **Kanhapo Kamukata ke dule to ende** – Putting more effort when doing something yields better results than doing it with minimal effort.

5. **Efundo ihali lingangele** – There is no way one can escape fate.

6. **Onhumba yeku dja oinyenga kulitenga** – It is difficult to hurt your relatives.

7. **Eulu kali na eegudi ngeno omapongo hatu londo** – Heaven does not have a ladder otherwise we the impoverished would use it to climb.

8. **Oiyuma I li elimba limwe ihai pu okupulungudja** – People who live together will always have misunderstandings or problems.

9. **Kalunga iha kwafa elai** – One must help himself or herself for God to help him or her.

10. **Kambungu hepa, mongula u ninge Shime shamakulumbungu** – A person who is poor today will have a better life tomorrow.

11. **Etimaumbwile oli dule ekuta** – Having hope is better than having temporary satisfaction.

12. **Kalunga oshiims eshi e ku nhunina ihe shi li po** – If God promises you something, it will come to pass.

13. **Omunhu e he ku lilile ke fi woye** – People ask for help from those they trust.

14. **Mukweni mu udila ta li, ino mu udila ta lili** — Help someone when they are in trouble, do not only help them when they are eating.

15. **Nekwa litoka oye ngoo nyoko** — Your mother is still your mother whether she is poor or ugly.

16. **Kalunga iha kwatelwa ta tenge** — When God is doing something, he does not need anyone's help.

17. **Oshiyuma shiwa ihashi kala limba** — A good person does not live long; he/she dies at an early age.

18. **E ku pa kashona e ku xunga omwenyo** — One who gives you little has nurtured your life.

19. **Uha pandula novake** — If you do not appreciate, you will end up stealing.

20. **Loshipute olo hali lika** — It is the one who has a certain weakness that gets accused a lot.

21. **Waalombwelwa noyi niiso paantu** — If you do not listen to good advice, you will be embarrassed in public.

22. **Omukulunhu okwa lya ohonde notwila** — Elders have encountered tribulations in life.

23. **Tashi ya ihashi londelwa, tashi i osho hashi talwa** — You can only see what is going but you cannot see what is coming because you do not know when it will come.

24. **Fo iha popi ngengo a londwela Mhanda** — Things do not speak otherwise they would warn people.

25. **Okambadwa kashona ke dule to nangala pedu** — Sleeping on a small blanket is better than sleeping on the floor.

NIGERIEN PROVERBS

Country: Niger

Capital City: Niamey

Area of Country: 1,267,000km²

Population: 27,448,106

Demonym: Nigerien

Currency: West African Franc (XOF)

Independence Day: 3rd August 1960

Official Language: French

National Languages: Hausa, Fulfulde, Arabic, Buduma, Fulfulde, Tebu, Kanuri, Zarma, Tassawaq, Songhai, Tamasheq

National Motto: Fraternity, Work, Progress

ABOUT HAUSA

Hausa is a Chadic language spoken by the Hausa people in Niger, Nigeria, and several other West African countries. It is one of the major languages in Niger, where it is primarily spoken in the regions of Zinder, Maradi, and Diffa.

HAUSA – ENGLISH

1. **Komin nisan jifa sai ta dawo kasa** – No matter how far a stone is, it will always come back down.

2. **Rua ba su yami banza** – Water does not get bitter without a cause.

3. **Ba'a damisa biyu a wuri, ko an yi guda ke daukan girma** – No two leopards can stay in one place and even if they do, one assumes leadership.

4. **A patient person will cook a stone and drink its broth** – Mai hakuri ya kan dafa dutse ya sha romonsa.

5. **Hannu d'aya ba ya d'aukar jinka** – One hand does not carry your feelings.

6. **Gaskiya daci gareta** – The truth is always bitter.

7. **Ba'a magaji da yaro** – A child cannot become an elder overnight.

8. **Abu ga hannu shi ne mutum** – An item in the hand is what makes one a person.

9. **Ba'a wane bakin banza** – People of substance are worth more than one can imagine.

10. **Abokin barawo, barawo ne** – The friend of a thief is a thief.

11. **Komai nisan dare gari zai waye** – No matter how long the night the day will break.

12. **Mahukurci mawadaci** – A patient person is a wealthy person.

13. **Sannu ba ta hana zuwa, in ji kunkuru** - Travelling slowly does not keep one from arriving, says the tortoise.

14. **Kwadayi mabudin wahala** - Greed is the key path to trouble.

15. **Zama lafiya yafi zama dan sarki** – It is better to live in peace than to be a prince.

16. **Sai an kula kashi yake doyi (wari)** - Silence is the best answer to a fool.

17. **Da wasa ake fadawa wawa magana** - A word is enough for the wise.

18. **Amfanin hankali aiki da shi** - The value of good sense is in making use of it.

19. **In za ka gina ramin mugunta gina shi gajere** — If you are going to dig a hole of wickedness, dig it shallow.

20. **Babu laifi, babu tunani** — If one does no wrong, there is no regret.

21. **Alla ya ce, Tashi in taimaka ka** — God says, get up, and then let me help you.

22. **Ba a hada gudu da susar katara** — It is impossible to race more than your speed.

23. **Tsare gaskiya ko da wuta aka saka ka** — Keep to the truth even if they put you in the fire.

24. **Hannu daya baya daukan jinka** — One hand cannot lift a hut.

25. **Kaso danuwanka kamar kanka** — Love your neighbour like yourself.

NIGERIAN PROVERBS

Country: Nigeria

Capital City: Abuja

Area of Country: 923,768km^2

Population: 225.077,176

Demonym: Nigerian

Currency: Nigerian Naira (NGN)

Independence Day: 1st October 1960

Official Language: English

National Languages: Hausa, Igbo, Yoruba

Other Languages Include: Fulani, Idoma, Ijaw, Edo, Nupe, Efik-Ibibio, Urhobo, Gbagyi, Tiv, Nupe, Isoko, Ukwuani

National Motto: Unity and Faith, Peace, and Progress

ABOUT YORUBA

Yoruba is a Niger-Congo language spoken primarily in southwestern Nigeria , including states like Lagos, Oyo, Ogun, Osun, and Ekiti. It is one of the largest ethnic groups in Nigeria, and the Yoruba language holds significant cultural and linguistic importance. Yoruba is also spoken in neighbouring countries such as Benin, Togo, and parts of Sierra Leone.

YORUBA – ENGLISH

1. **Tí ewé gbígbẹ bá bọ́ lára igi, ó nkọ ewé tútù lógbọ́n ni** - A dry leaf that falls off a tree serves as a lesson to the fresh ones.

2. **Ẹ̀dá ò l'áròpin / -** No one can be written off.

3. **Òjò tó rò sí ewúro, náà ló rò sí ìrèké / -** The same rain that fell on the bitter-leaf, fell on the sugarcane.

4. **Òkò àbínújù kì í pẹyẹ -** A stone thrown in anger does not kill a bird.

5. **A kì í nìkan jayé -** One does not enjoy life alone.

6. **Ọgbọ́n díẹ̀ agọ̀ díẹ̀, l'ẹ̀dá fi ńrí ilé ayé gbé; ọgbọ́n àgbọ́njù a máa pa ọlọ́gbọ́n lára / -** A little wisdom combined with a little stupidity is how anyone gets to live in the world; excessive wisdom often proves harmful to the carrier in the end.

7. **Ojú ẹni máa là, á rí íyọnu / -** Whoever desires success will experience challenges.

8. **Ẹ̀ní máa jẹ oyin inú àpáta kìí wo ẹnu àáké -** Whoever will eat the honey from a rock does not worry about the edge of the axe.

9. **Òkun kì í hó ruru, kí á wà á ruru / -** Do not paddle wildly in a stormy sea.

10. **Àfopiná tóní òun ó pa fìtìlà, ara ẹ ni yóò pa -** A moth that attempts to put out the burning fire in a lamp will only kill itself.

11. **Dídùn ló dùn tá ńbá ọ̀rẹ́ jẹ ẹ̀kọ; ti ilé oge to óge é jẹ -** We eat with a friend because of the pleasure of friendship not because we lack.

12. **Gbangba l'àṣá ń ta -** The hawk always spreads its wings to the fullest.

13. **Ìgbín ò lè sáré bí Ajá; ìyẹn ò ní kó máà de ibi tó ńlọ / -** The snail is truly not as fast as the dog; yet this will not stop the snail from getting to its destination.

14. **Ibi tí a gbé epo sí a kì í sọ òkò síbè -** One does not throw rocks at the place where one has one's palm-oil stored.

15. **Gbogbo ẹni tó di ojú kọ́ ló ńsùn; gbogbo ojú tí a là sílẹ̀ kọ́ ló ńríran** - Not all those who close their eyes are sleeping; not all eyes that are wide open are seeing.

16. **Tí owó ò bá tí ì dé ọwọ̀ èyàn, ìwà oníwà ló máa máa hù** / - You will never know who anyone really is until he or she becomes wealthy.

17. **Alágbára má mèrò baba ọ̀lẹ** / - To be strong but lack wisdom is the height of indolence.

18. **Gbogbo ọ̀rọ̀ kọ́ là ńfí ẹnu sọ** - It's not all matters that are expressed verbally.

19. **Èèyàn boni lára jaṣọ lọ; ẹni tó láṣọ tí ò léèyàn, ìhòhò ló wà.** / - People provide better cover than clothes; whoever has clothes but has no one, is naked.

20. **Ohun tí a kò jẹ lẹ́nu kì í rùn lọ́nà ọ̀fun ẹni** / - What one has not eaten cannot be reflected in one's breath.

21. **Bí ó ti lè wù kí oòrùn mú gangan tó, bó pẹ́ bó yá, ó ńbọ̀ wá fi àyè sílẹ̀ fún òṣùpá** / - No matter how hot the sun is up above, eventually it will leave room for the moon.

22. **Yàrá kótópó gba ogún ọ̀rẹ́, bí ìfẹ́ bá wà láàárín in wọn** / - A little room is good enough for 20 friends, if there is love amongst them.

23. **Àmójúkúrò ni í mú ẹ̀mí ìfẹ́ gùn** / - Willingness to overlook is what makes loving relationships endure.

24. **Ìwà kì í fi oníwà sílẹ̀** / - We are inseparable from our character.

25. **Ẹni èyàn ò kí kó yọ̀; ẹni Ọlọ́run ò kí kó ṣọ́ra** / - Those shunned by man should rejoice; but those shunned by God should be worried.

RWANDAN PROVERBS

Country: Rwanda

Capital City: Kigali

Area of Country: 26,338km²

Population: 14,170,930

Demonyms: Rwandan, Rwandese

Currency: Rwandan Franc (RWF)

Independence Day: 1st July 1962

Official Languages: Kinyarwanda, Swahili, French, English

National Motto: Unity, Work, Patriotism

ABOUT KINYARWANDA

Kinyarwanda also known as Rwanda-Rundi, is a Bantu language which is the mother tongue of most of the Rwandan population. It is also spoken by some communities in eastern Congo, particularly in the Kivu region, and in parts of Uganda.

KINYARWANDA - ENGLISH

1. **Akabi gasekwa nkakeza** - Even the unfortunate is laughable.

2. **Umwana w umufundi arabwirirwa ntaburara** - A child of a skilled workman does not sleep with an empty stomach.

3. **Agati gateretswe n'Imana ntigahungabanywa n'umuyaga** - The tree planted by God is not shaken by the wind.

4. **Ujya kwica ubukombe arabwagaza** – The smart one gives in.

5. **Umuntu ananira umuhana nta we unanira umushuka** - You can resist whoever advises you but not whoever lies to you.

6. **Umugani ntuva ku busa** - A proverb never comes from nowhere.

7. **Umushitsi ni nkuruze ruhita mugihe gito** - Visitors are like streams that pass for a while.

8. **Ababiri bishe umwe** - Two are better than one.

9. **Mweshobora urenga aho kwirukanu mwe ariko ntabwo aho kwirukanu mu matimu wawe** - You can outdistance that which is running after you, but not what is running inside you.

10. **Ryari mweukwata inzika, anyu umwana gukwata inzika kandi** – When you bear a grudge, your child will also bear a grudge.

11. **Uwanze guhingira inyoni yiyicisha inzara** – He who sows reap.

12. **Aho kwica gitera uzice ikibimutera** – Hate the sin, love the sinner.

13. **Ingunga y'urulimi inesha injunga z'igitero** – The sharpness of the tongue defeats the sharpness of the warriors.

14. **Amaziro n'amaciro birangana** – Ends and beginnings are identical.

15. **Akarênze impinga karushya ihámagara** – When what is said reaches the top of the hill, it cannot be called back.

16. **Nta muhanuzi mu babo** – No prophet amongst ourselves.

17. **Umusonga w'ûndi ntûkubúza gusinzìra** – Someone else's stomach ache does not prevent you from sleeping.

18. **Ifumbire y'úbucuti ni âmagambo** – The fertiliser of friendship is made with words.

19. **Aho ujishe igisabo ntuhatera ibuye** — You should never bite the hand that feeds you.

20. **Ukiranutse na bene amasaka yubaka ikigega** — He who pays his debts is rich.

21. **Agapfundikiye gatera amatsiko** — Simplicity is the best policy.

22. **Kugenda cyane gutera kubona** — If you walk a lot, you see a lot.

23. **Nyir'ubwenge aruta nyir'uburyo** — Knowledge is better than wealth.

24. **Ihene mbi ntuyizirikaho iyawe** — Bad company leads to trouble.

25. **Iby 'ejo bibara ab'ejo** — Tomorrow's things are told by those coming tomorrow.

SÃO TOMÉAN PROVERBS

Country: São Tomé and Príncipe

Capital City: São Tomé

Area of Country: 1,001km²

Population: 232,959

Demonyms: São Toméan, Santomean

Currency: São Tomé and Príncipe Dobra (STN)

Independence Day: 12th July 1975

Official Language: Portuguese

Other Languages Include: Forro Creole (Sãotomense) Angolar Creole (N'gola), Principense Creole (Lunguyê)

National Motto: Unity, Discipline, Labour

ABOUT FORRO CREOLE (SÃOTOMENSE)

Forro Creole, also known as Sãotomense or São Toméan Creole, is a creole language and is the native language of many São Toméans. Forro Creole is primarily based on Portuguese, but it has been significantly influenced by African languages and cultures. It incorporates African vocabulary, grammar, and pronunciation.

FORRO CREOLE (SÃOTOMENSE) – ENGLISH

1. **Omali sa stlagado magi pixe cu sa nê sa ximple** - The sea is salty, but the fish that live in it are simple.

2. **Lopa malich ê ka cotá ni códó** – He who acts out of evil faith will have an evil end.

3. **Tudu nguê cu ka ximiá ventu, ê ka coiê tlóvada** — Whoever sows winds reaps storms.

4. **Tudu kwa ku ka luji na sa ôlo fa** - Everything that shines is not gold.

5. **Bana bôbô ê na ta ka bila kulu fa** — Ripe bananas will never be raw again.

6. **Olha fyô pasa bon vida** — A cool head is greater than a good life.

7. **Home mon bétu só ka tadá cu muala** — Only the generous man lives longer than his wife.

8. **Fala tendê na ka ba wê de suxi fa** — Hearing something is not worth much in the eyes of a judge.

9. **Kolê flontadu na sa tê fa** — Sacrificing so much is not synonymous with gaining.

10. **Manda ka fia ope, maji ê na ka fia kloson fa** - Sending (a message) eases the feet, but not the heart.

11. **Blublublu na sa luta fa** - Having everything in haste does not work.

12. **Dedu na ka ponta ubwê dê fa, se ya na lá** — The finger does not point to itself, always the other.

13. **Sangue na sa awa fa** — Blood is not water.

14. **Migu d'ome sa kloson dê** — Man's friend is his heart.

15. **Ngê cu a ka fla nê soku ka tê vida lôngo** — Whoever is talked about a lot will have a long life.

16. **Bô na nancê ku kwa fa, bô na ka molê lêlê fa** — You were not born with wealth, you will no die because of it.

17. **Kukunudu na sa tason fa** — Stooping is not sitting.

18. **Tudu dentxi betu na sa gôxto fa** – All laughter does not mean joy.

19. **Ngê na te lolozu fa ká vija plama ni blaku** – People who do not have a watch discover dawn in a hole.

20. **Tudu nguê ca plemê tê vonté di loló dédu** – Everyone who squeezes honey wants to lick their fingers.

21. **Txi ka ta ichima oriô passa, txi ká vê musca qui tê koni** - If you sit on faeces for a long time, you will end up seeing flies.

22. **Cavalu di quato opé machi pô cu san biogó fá kantu machi ami qui tê dôçu?** - If the horse that has four legs cannot stand on the slippery ground, how much more me that only has two?

23. **Cabeça na pensa fa clôpô ca toma chicotxi** – When the head does not regulate the body, it's what pays.

24. **Cucúndia nacê fimi, muê tôto** – The coconut tree is born straight and dies crooked.

25. **Kwa de tê ka bi ni mon di dêsu** – Gains come from the hand of God.

SENEGALESE PROVERBS

Country: Senegal
Capital City: Dakar
Area of Country: 196,839km²
Population: 17,875,660
Demonym: Senegalese
Currency: West African Franc (XOF)
Independence Day: 4th April 1960
Official Language: French
National Languages: Wolof, Arabic, Pulaar, Serer, Diola, Malinke
National Motto: One People, One Goal, One Faith

ABOUT WOLOF

Wolof is a prominent Niger-Congo language in Senegal, where it is the native tongue of the Wolof people. It is widely spoken in urban and rural areas and plays a significant role in Senegal's cultural and linguistic landscape. Wolof is also spoken in neighbouring countries, including Gambia and Mauritania.

WOLOF - ENGLISH

1. **Bàlà ngâ fajan, fajal sa bopà** - Before taking up the profession of healing, heal yourself.

2. **Hamul ây nà, vandé lâjtéul a ko rav** - Not knowing is bad, but not asking is worse.

3. **Dàv, rav ci ngör là bokà** - Running away, escaping is part of courage.

4. **Dekando bu bâh a gen mbokà mu soré** - A good neighbour is better than a distant relative.

5. **Ku vor ku la dul or, Yalla vor la** - He who betrays someone who does not betray him, God will betray him.

6. **Ku sângô der, nà votu jégi safarà** - He who is covered with seeded cotton must be careful not to step over the fire.

7. **Lu nar héyéhéy, bu degà gà gonenté jot ko** - No matter how early the lie, if the truth rises in the evening, it will reach it.

8. **Ku Yalla sani fità, dô ko màn a fàku** - He to whom God throws a dart cannot avoid it.

9. **Ku sa begé baré, sa ngor név** - He who desires too much has little honour.

10. **Gacê'k hâmadi, lâjul a ko indi** - Shame and ignorance are the share of those who do not ask.

11. **Ñètà i lonkà bènà du cà fakhà: lunk'u jigèn, lunk'u bûr fari, ak lunk'u jiné** - There are three bonds that are difficult to break: the bond of a woman, the bond of a great king and the bond of a genius.

12. **Ku ôlu Yalla, di nga vèr** - He who trusts in God will succeed.

13. **Ham sa bopà mô gen ku la ko vah** - Knowing yourself is better than learning it from someone else.

14. **Bàlà ngâ oyu nèka fà** - Before answering the call, you must be present.

15. **Lô ragal-ragal, sa tat fété ca génav** - No matter how much you fear, your behind is always behind.

16. **Vah i mag doyul à védi** - We must not contradict the words of the old men.

17. **Fu jinah yabé mûs, mpah a fà jêgèñ** - Where the mouse braves the cat, there is a hole nearby.

18. **Lô têl-têl à jog, yôn jîtu la** - No matter how early you get up, the path precedes you.

19. **Ku di, lô begà, jâr cà, sa ngor yahu** - He who wants to obtain everything he desires, loses honesty.

20. **Ku bidanté hif** - Laziness breeds misery.

21. **Jadà, bûr fari là** - Satisfying one's natural needs is a powerful king.

22. **Bô gisé ku dèf lu mu varul à dèf, bul ko farfarlé** - If you see someone doing what they should not do, do not embolden him by joining his side.

23. **Lu vagajâné mayé du and'ak njériñ** - What one obtains by illicit means does not benefit.

24. **Dar jantà bà fènkà** - Covering the sun with your hands won't stop it from rising.

25. **Adunà ñèt'a cê gen : am a gen, men a gen, ham a gen** - Three things prevail on earth: owning, power and knowledge.

SEYCHELLOIS PROVERBS

Country: Seychelles

Capital City: Victoria

Area of Country: 455km^2

Population: 107,811

Demonyms: Seychellois, Seychelloise

Currency: Seychelles Rupee (SCR)

Independence Day: 29th June 1976

Official Languages: English, French, Seychellois Creole (Seselwa Kreol)

National Motto: The end crowns the work.

ABOUT SESELWA KREOL

Seselwa Kreol, also known as Seychellois Creole or simply Kreol, is the mother tongue of most of the population in the Seychelles. It is the most widely spoken language in the country and serves as the lingua franca. Seselwa Kreol emerged as a means of communication among the diverse population, incorporating French, African languages, and other influences.

SESELWA KREOL – ENGLISH

1. **En sak vid pa kapab rete dibou** - An empty bag cannot stand.

2. **En hash i kapab bliye, me pye dibwa pou toultan mazinen -** The axe forgets but the tree remembers.

3. **Pa tou bon lezo ki tonm dan lagel en bon lisyen** - Not every good dog gets a good bone.

4. **Si ou kras dan lezer i a tonm lo ou menm** - If you spit up, it will fall back on you.

5. **Delo lo fey sonz** – Like water on a taro leaf.

6. **Zako i war lake son kanmarad, i pa war sa ki pour li** - A monkey sees its neighbour's tail and not its own.

7. **Ou pa kapab kaka pli gro ki ou trou deryer** - You cannot excrete much bigger than your anus.

8. **San-t-an pour le voler, en zour pour le met** – A hundred days for the thief, one day for the owner.

9. **Dibri lanmer pa anpes pti pwason dormi** - The noise of the sea does not stop the fish from sleeping.

10. **Lonm propoz, Dye dispoz** - Man proposes, God disposes.

11. **Boulwar pa kapab dir marmit i nwanr** - The kettle cannot call the pot black.

12. **Labou pa kapab riy lanmar** - Mud cannot laugh at the marsh.

13. **Gard lalang pour manz diri** - Keep the tongue to eat rice with.

14. **Sa ki ou zet ek lipye, ou anmas ek lalang** - What you discard with your foot, you retrieve with your tongue.

15. **Si ou frekant lisyen, ou bezwen ganny pis** - When you keep company with dogs, you can expect to catch fleas.

16. **Zwazo menm nik i kouv menm dizef** - Birds of the same nest lay the same eggs.

17. **Dibwa tord i devin dwat dan dife** – Crooked wood is straightened with fire.

18. **I pa vo lapenn vid plis delo dan losean** – It is not worth adding water to the sea.

19. **Zis vre zanmi ki pou dir ou si ou figir i sal** – Real friends tell you when your face is dirty.

20. **Mars dan ou savat ziskan ler ou trouv ou soulye** – Walk in your slippers until you can find your shoes.

21. **Lizye i zanmen bliy sa ki leker in vwar** – The heart never forgets what the heart has seen.

22. **Zako I sot zis distans ki i konnen I kapab sote** – The monkey leaps only as far as it can reach.

23. **Ler ou tyonbo ou prop delo, ki ou pou mazin sak gout** – Once you carry your own water, you will remember every drop..

24. **He who looks for honey must have the courage to face the bees** – Sa ki pe rod lemiel, bezwen annan kouraz pou fas bann abey.

25. **Si ou kwar ou tro pti pou fer en diferans, sey dormi aswar avek en sel moustik** – If you think you are too small to make a difference, try spending the night with a mosquito.

SIERRA LEONEAN PROVERBS

Country: Sierra Leone

Capital City: Freetown

Area of Country: 71,740km²

Population: 8,838,117

Demonym: Sierra Leonean

Currency: Sierra Leonean Leone (SLE)

Independence Day: 27th April 1961

Official Language: English

National Language: Sierra Leonean Creole (Krio)

Other Languages Include: Kono, Temne, Mende, Fula, Maninka, Pular, Sherbro, Sua, Limba, Loko, Kissi, Kuranko, Klao, Yalunka

National Motto: Unity, Freedom, Justice

ABOUT SIERRA LEONEAN CREOLE (KRIO)

Sierra Leonean Creole, commonly referred to as Krio, is a Creole language widely spoken in Sierra Leone. Krio developed when natives returned to Sierra Leone from the Americas, particularly Nova Scotia in Canada. Krio incorporates English, African languages, and elements from other languages.

SIERRA LEONEAN CREOLE (KRIO) – ENGLISH

1. **Gɛt-gɛt nɔ want, want-want nɔ gɛt** – He who has does not want, he who wants does not have.

2. **Fambul tik kin bɛn, bɔt i nɔba brok** - The family tree may bend, but it never breaks.

3. **Wata we yu nɔ fred, na de yu go lɛf** - The water that you are not afraid of is where you'll drown.

4. **Gɔd go bɔta mi bred** – God will butter my bread.

5. **Yu yon dɔl kɔtlas bɛtɛ pas yu neba shap wan** - Your own dull machete is better than your neighbour's sharp one.

6. **We dɛn tot yu na bak, yu nɔ no se rod langga** - If they carry you on their back, you will not know that the road is long.

7. **Bɔl-ed man nɔba ambɔg hɔni** - A bald man never aggravates bees.

8. **Hat nɔto bon** - The heart is not made of bone.

9. **Udat tredin wit gɔd nɔba lɔs** - He who trades with God never loses.

10. **Di san de kɔmɔt tu-tu** - The sun comes out twice.

11. **If yu want ɔl, yu de lɔs ɔl** - If you want everything, you will lose everything.

12. **Yu go cham fɔ pɔsin, bɔt yu nɔ go swala fɔ-ram** - You can chew for a person, but you cannot swallow for him.

13. **Gɔd, we gi man krɔ-krɔ, na-in gi am han fɔ krach am** - God, who gave man scabies, also gave him hands to scratch them.

14. **Dis laif wi lib: nɛks wɔl nɔ go tan so** - This life that we live: The next world will not be so.

15. **If yu bit fɔ kresman, yusɛf kres** - If you beat the drum for a madman, you are crazy too.

16. **Yu kɔba smok sote, i mɔs kɔmɔt** - No matter how much you try to cover up smoke, it must come out.

17. **If yu listin pan makit nois, yu nɔ go bai wetin yu want** - If you listen to the market's noise, you will not buy what you want.

18. **Sabi nɔ gɛt wɔri** - Knowledge has no worry.

19. **ɔl mɔta-man nɔ ikwa na dis wɔl, na-in mek fingga dɛnsɛf nɔ ikwa** — Not everyone is equal in this world, in the same way that fingers are not of equal size.

20. **Pikin big sote, i nɔ go big pas in papa** - No matter how big a child is, he will never be bigger than his father.

21. **As yu sɛl yusɛf, na so di wɔl go bai yu** - As you sell yourself, so the world will buy you.

22. **If yu sabi was yu han, yu kin it wit big pipul dɛn** - If you know how to wash your hands you can eat with important people.

23. **If yu trowe asis, asis go fala yu** - If you throw ashes, ashes will follow you.

24. **Wetin gɔd dɔn plant, yu nɔ gɛt fɔ wata-ram** - When God has planted something, you do not have to water it.

25. **Rod lɔng te, i de ɛnd pan tɔn (na pan tɔn i de stɔp** - No matter how long the road, it ends at a town.

SOMALI PROVERBS

Country: Somalia
Capital City: Mogadishu
Area of Country: 637,655km^2
Population: 18,285,832
Demonym: Somali
Currency: Somali Shilling (SOS)
Independence Day: 1st July 1960
Official Language: Somali, Arabic
Other Languages Include: Garra, Oromo, Boon, Mushunguli

ABOUT SOMALI

Somali is an Afroasiatic (Cushitic branch) language spoken primarily in the Horn of Africa, particularly in Somalia, Somaliland, and parts of Ethiopia, Djibouti, and Kenya. Somali diaspora communities can be found in various countries around the world.

SOMALI - ENGLISH

1. **Intaanad fallin ka fiirso** – Look before you leap.

2. **Hadal waa mergi hadba meel u jiidma** – Talk is like a tendon that can be moved to different places.

3. **Qof aan dhididin ma dhergo** – A person who has not sweated does not get their fill.

4. **Dhar aanad lahayni dhaxan kaama cesho** – Somebody else's clothes do not warm you.

5. **Gar iyo geeri loo siman** – People are equal when it comes to justice and death.

6. **Rag haween ayaa kala hor mariya** – It is the women who make some men succeed where others fail.

7. **Talo xumo tog baas bay kaa riddaa** – Bad counsel may cause you to fall into abyss.

8. **Aqoon la'aan wa iftin la'aan** – Lack of knowledge is lack of light.

9. **Eebe ma naxee waa naxariistaa** – God does not have mercy but is merciful.

10. **Doqonnimo daawo ma leh** – One cannot be cured of foolishness.

11. **Shimbiri laba geed ma wada gurato** – A bird cannot eat from two trees at the same time.

12. **Nabad la'ani waa nolol la'an** – Without peace there is no life.

13. **Qunyar socde qodax ma mudo** – He who walks slowly will not get pricked by a thorn.

14. **Kibir waa lagu kufaa** – Arrogance can trip you up.

15. **Sirow ma hodmo** – A deceiver never prospers.

16. **Aadmi la aragyaaba, dhib la arag** – People are seen, problems are not seen.

17. **Beentaada hore runtaada danbay u baas baxdaa** – Your previous lie damages your present truth.

18. **Gogol rag waa godob la'aan** – A good conscience is a soft pillow.

19. **Hadduusan qadhaadh jireen, miyaa la qiri lahaa malab** – Who has never tasted bitter, knows not what is sweet.

20. **Ilko wada jir wax ku gooyaan** — Teeth cut something together.

21. **Khayr wax kaama dhimmee, shar u toog hay** — Hope for the best and prepare for the worst.

22. **Hawl karnimo waa hooyada hannaanka guusha** - Diligence is the mother of success.

23. **Ama waa la muuqdaa, ama waa la maqnaada** — Either be visible or be absent.

24. **Ballandarro waa diindarro** — Not fulfilling a promise is the same as not believing in God.

25. **Aaddane eed ma waayo** — Human beings are never without a fault.

SOUTH AFRICAN PROVERBS

Country: South Africa
Capital Cities: Cape Town (Legislative), Pretoria (Executive),
Bloemfontein (Judicial)
Area of Country: 1,221,000km²
Population: 60,568,926
Demonym: South African
Currency: South African Rand (ZAR)
Freedom Day: 27ᵗʰ April 1994
Official Languages: isiZulu, Afrikaans, English, isiNdebele, isiXhosa,
Sesotho, Sesotho sa Leboa (Sepedi), Setswana, SiSwati, Tshivenda,
Xitsonga
Other Languages Include: Silala, isiHlubi, KheLobedu, SePulana,
Khoekhoegowab, SiPhuti,
National Motto: Diverse people unite.

ABOUT ISIZULU

Zulu, also known as isiZulu, is a Bantu language spoken primarily in the KwaZulu-Natal province of South Africa, where the Zulu people are the largest ethnic group. It is also spoken in neighbouring regions and by Zulu diaspora communities.

ISIZULU – ENGLISH

1. **Amakhonco akhala emabili** – Two heads are better than one.

2. **Ingane engakhali ifela embelekweni** – One who does not ask for help will be overcome by his own challenges.

3. **Akundlovu yasindwa umboko wayo** – No elephant was ever inconvenienced by its trunk.

4. **Inxeba lendoda alihlekwa** – Do not celebrate someone else's misfortune.

5. **Akwaziwa mbhantshi kujiya** – We do not know what is going to happen.

6. **Inyoni ishayelwa abakhulu** – When you are successful remember those who put you there.

7. **Ayinuki ingosiwe** – Rumours always come from a certain truth.

8. **Ithi ingahamba idle udaka** – Beggars cannot be choosers.

9. **Ayikho inkomo yobuthongo** – You cannot earn cows while sleeping.

10. **Ohlab eyake kalelwa** – He who slaughters his own beast is not forbidden.

11. **Libunjwa lis eva** – The day is worked while it is still fresh.

12. **Umuntu ngumuntu ngabantu** – A person is a person because of people.

13. **Zonke iziziba zogcwala inhlabathi** – All rivers will be filled with soil.

14. **Kumbamba ezingelayo** – Your desire to achieve something must be matched by your effort to achieve it.

15. **Indlela ibuza kwabaphambili** – The way forward is to ask those who have been before.

16. **Sihlahla saziwa ngezithelo zaso** - A tree is known by its fruit.

17. **Inyoni ishayelwa abadala** – Elders will reap the fruits of their generations.

18. **Iso liwela umfula ugcwele** — The eye crosses the full river.

19. **Ubude abupangwa** — Height is not achieved in a hurry.

20. **Aku langa litshona lingena ndaba zalo** — There is no sun that sets without its affairs.

21. **Ukupa kuzibekela** - To give is to provide for one-self.

22. **Aku nyoka yakohlwa umgodi wayo** — No snake ever forgot its own hole.

23. **Inkunzi isematholeni** — The bull is amongst the calves.

24. **Inxeba lendoda alihlekwa** — The wound of a man is not laughed at.

25. **Nula kungekho ghude liyasa** — Even when the rooster is not present, day dawns.

SOUTH SUDANESE PROVERBS

Country: South Sudan

Capital City: Juba

Area of Country: 644,329km^2

Population: 11,137,164

Demonym: South Sudanese

Currency: South Sudanese Pound (SSP)

Independence Day: 9th July 2011

Official Language: English

National Languages Include: Nuer, Lopit, Bari, Dinka, Luwo, Murle, Zande, Pari, Ma'di, Otuho, Masalit, Fallata, Koalib, Toposa, Hausa, Shilluk and more. *(All indigenous languages of South Sudan are classed as national languages.)*

Other Languages Include: Juba Arabic

National Motto: Justice, Liberty, Prosperity

ABOUT NUER

Nuer is a Nilo-Saharan language spoken primarily by the Nuer people in South Sudan, as well as in some regions of Ethiopia and Sudan. It is one of the Nuer-Kordofanian languages and is known for its complex system of nouns and verbal morphology. Historically, Nuer was primarily an oral language, and it did not have a widely used writing system. In recent years, efforts have been made to develop a written form of Nuer using the Latin script.

NUER – ENGLISH

1. **/Ca puɔth kuany piny** - The blessing (your fate or destiny) is not chosen.

2. **Bak cäŋɔ kɛ bakdɛ** - Each day dawns in its way.

3. **Ɣɛl gɔaal thilɛ mal** - There is no peace in eating alone.

4. **Yil yiil jekɛ guandɛ** - Doubts catch the hesitant person.

5. **Tëk ɛ walɛ mɛ, ɛ duɔɔp tëkä mi ruɔn ɔ** - Today's life makes the path for tomorrow.

6. **/Cu rɔ bi nyaany cɔaat** - Do not remain on the riverbank.

7. **Thilɛ ram yiëë kɛ wum raam min dɔŋ** - No one breathes with the nose of another person.

8. **Ram mi thiec duɔp, /cɛ dee bath** - The person who asks directions will not get lost.

9. **Thiɛlɛ mi bëë kɛ pek** - Nothing will not come to an end.

10. **Kuoth ɛ kuur** - God is a craftsman.

11. **Ram mi lät tɛth lɔcdɛ, ku talaŋ lɛ göri thuk naath** - The man who works rejoices, whereas the lazy one gives troubles to people.

12. **Riaŋ kuic ɛ ŋak, kä buɔth nooŋɛ car** - Riches know nothing whereas famine offers a thought.

13. **Nyuään jakɛ kak kä wä juɔl** - Laziness makes the garden get plenty of weeds.

14. **/Ca wäl math baaŋ** - The medicine is not drunk free.

15. **Goor ciok rɔl ikä** - The leg looks after the throat.

16. **Guɛc lenyɛ liɛm** - Seeking is better than begging.

17. **Min pen ji niɛn tuok tharɛ jin** - What prevents you from sleeping comes from within.

18. **Mi jali kɛɛl kɛ kuel dɔpi kuel** - If you walk together with thieves you learn theft.

19. **Gaat kɛ kuaay ti ruun ti** - Children are the seeds of the future.

20. **/Cu rɔ jiop kak mi /cị bi luäŋ kɛ puɔr** - Do not clean a field that you will not be able to cultivate.

21. **/Ci Ɣöth thokdɛ tee kacä** - Changing your mind is not being a liar.

22. **Cioor lɔaac noŋɛ thil lieŋ** - Blindness of the heart brings misunderstanding.

23. **/C riɛk wun cẹtkɛ nhiaal** - Problems cannot be foreseen like the coming of the rain.

24. **/Cu riẹt yor cẹtkɛ with war** - Do not throw words like a stick in the night.

25. **/Ci run diaal cẹtkɛ cuëëk** - Years are not like twins.

SUDANESE PROVERBS

Country: Sudan

Capital City: Khartoum

Area of Country: 1,886,068km²

Population: 48.429,159

Demonyms: Sudanese

Currency: Sudanese Pound (SDG)

Independence Day: 1ˢᵗ January 1956

Official Languages: Arabic, English

National Languages: Sudanese Arabic

Other Languages Include: Domari, Hausa, Lafofa, Tama, Tumtum, Kanga, Yulu

National Motto: Victory is ours.

ABOUT SUDANESE ARABIC

Sudanese Arabic, also known as Juba Arabic, is a colloquial Arabic dialect spoken primarily in Sudan, particularly in the capital city of Khartoum and other urban areas. It is distinct from Standard Arabic and has unique linguistic features influenced by other languages spoken in Sudan.

SUDANESE ARABIC – ENGLISH

1. **Al-ta'leam ma a'indu a'umur** - There is no age for learning.

2. **Al-a'ilm silah'** - Knowledge is a weapon.

3. **Darb al-salama lil h'ul gareab** - A safe road is short even if it takes a year to walk it.

4. **Al-s'ah kan ma najjak al-kid'ib ma binaji** - If telling the truth does not save you, lies will not save you.

5. **Al-ma ghilit ma ita'alam** - He who makes no mistakes makes nothing.

6. **Katarat al-nagir kamalat al-h'ajar** - Constant digging finishes the stone.

7. **Al-moat bisawi bean al-ghani wa al-faqear** - Death makes the rich and the poor equal.

8. **A'duan beain wala s'adiqan munafiq** - Better an open enemy than a hypocritical friend.

9. **Al-biyan bil al-a'mal** - Deeds not words.

10. **Al-duniya bil-manafia' wa al-akhra bi-ala a'mal** - Life's benefit is in its opportunities, but afterlife's benefit is gained with good deeds.

11. **Beeran tishrab minu ma tarmi fihu wasakh** - Cast no dirt into the well that gives you water.

12. **Yitabia' a'ub al-nas wa yisawi al-aswa** - He who finds faults with others does worse himself.

13. **Al-khalaf ma mat** - He who leaves children never dies.

14. **Fagrean min al-dayan ghani** - A poor man without debt is rich.

15. **Al-ma bih'mal al-faqur ma bih'mal al-ghina** - He who does not endure poverty will not endure wealth.

16. **Al-faqur ma daim wa al-ghina ma daim** - Neither poverty nor wealth last long.

17. **Al-ma nas'ah'ak khanak** - He who does not advise you has betrayed you.

18. **Al-mabi al-s'uloh' nadman** - He who rejects reconciliation will regret it.

19. **La tabkhal bimawjoad wa la titkalaf bima'doam** - Do not be stingy with what you have and do not burden yourself with what you do not have.

20. **Arh'amo mann fi al-ard' yarh'mkum mann fi al-sama** - Show mercy to those who are on earth: He who is in heaven will have mercy upon you.

21. **Al-as'bba' al-wah'id ma bighat'i al-wajih** - One finger will not cover the face.

22. **Aa'tar birijlak ma taa'tar bilisanak** - Stumble with your foot; do not stumble with your tongue.

23. **Al-s'abr yihid al-jibal** - Patience demolishes mountains.

24. **Galeali wa la katear gheari** - The few that I have is better than the plenty that others have.

25. **Kan s'ifat al-niyah al-a'ngreab yisheel miyeah** - If people's intentions are sincere towards each other, one bed is enough for a hundred of them.

SWAZI PROVERBS

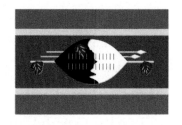

Country: Eswatini
Capital Cities: Mbabane (Executive), Lobamba (Legislative)
Area of Country: 17,364km²
Population: 1,213,665
Demonyms: Swazi
Currency: Swazi lilangeni (SZL)
Independence Day: 6ᵗʰ September 1968
Official Languages: Swazi, English
Other Languages Include: Zulu, Tsonga, Afrikaans
National Motto: We are the fortress.

ABOUT SWAZI

Swazi, also known as siSwati, is a Bantu (Nguni group) language spoken primarily in Eswatini. The language is also spoken in some regions of South Africa, particularly in the Mpumalanga and KwaZulu-Natal provinces. Swazi is closely related to Zulu and Xhosa.

SWAZI - ENGLISH

1. **Umuntu asikho ongakwazi ukufunda** – There is no one who cannot learn.

2. **Nga bw'otamalira, bw'otamala** – If you seek advice, take it all.

3. **Okubuza kuneneera** – Asking clarifies things.

4. **Kubona kanye kubona kabili** - To see once is to see twice.

5. **Emacili akalali endlini yinye** - Crafty people do not share the same house.

6. **Umuntu angeke aphile ngokuphuma endleleni** – A person cannot live by running away from problems.

7. **Indlela ibutwa kulabasembili** – Ask directions from those in front of you.

8. **Liso liwela umfula ugcwele** – Our wishes surpass our reality.

9. **Emandla endvodza akapheli** – The strength of a man has no ending.

10. **Sihlanya lomlomo beka ngaswane** – Silence is a shield against the evil tongue.

11. **Inkomo yemadvodza ingawungcole** – A cow that belongs to everyone will not be fat.

12. **Okubonera ku mabega, okwawula ku mubiri** - Seeing someone's back does not mean you know their body.

13. **Mafutsa lapho asitsandzeki khona akasafika** – A guest does not come to a place where he is not welcome.

14. **Mentiwa akakhohlwa, kukhohlwa menti** - The one offended never forgets and the offender forgets.

15. **Ubuti bubuyiselwa emhlane** – Good deeds are rewarded in the afterlife.

16. **Indlela yokufika emzini ayiphi** – There is no one way to get to the village.

17. **Ubuti buyabuya** – Goodness will return.

18. **Umuntu angahloniphi umntu akahloniphiwa** - A person who does not respect, will not be respected.

19. **Ukutsandza umuntwankulu kungakusiza** – Respecting elders will help you.

20. **Umuntu angaphahla ngabantu** – A person does not rely on people.

21. **Inhliziyo yakho ingakhuluma ngento enye, kodwa umlomo wakho ungatsho okunye** - Your heart can say one thing, but your mouth can say another.

22. **Ayena munawo, kutuma nayile** – The eye sees, but the heart knows.

23. **Ukuthanda kuyadlula ukuphila** – Love surpasses life.

24. **Omuliro gwayogerako, kimbuzi gyogerayo** – The fire you start will burn you too.

25. **Amateeka gamala g'agwo, amabeere g'amwa** – The teachings of your parents are your mirror.

TANZANIAN PROVERBS

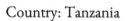

Country: Tanzania

Capital City: Dodoma

Area of Country: 945,087 km²

Population: 67,950,477

Demonyms: Tanzanian

Currency: Tanzanian Shilling (TZS)

Independence Day: 9th December 1961

Official Languages: Swahili, English, Arabic (Zanzibar)

Other Languages Include: Chasu, Zigula, Maa, Datooga, Ogiek, Digo, Kisankasa, Hehe

National Motto: Freedom and Unity

ABOUT PARE

Pare, also known as Kpare, Chasu, Asu, Athu or Kipare, is a Bantu language spoken in Tanzania. The language is spoken by The Pare people who are members of an indigenous ethnic group which inhabit the Pare Mountains of northern Tanzania, Mwanga and Same districts, Manyara, Tanga and, Kilimanjaro Region. The language has two dialects – Gonja and Mbaga.

PARE - ENGLISH

1. **Zunyoghememeya ujolya nemaja** – The patient man eats ripe fruit.

2. **Wunyodiofundusya na nyinya ugukundusya nang'ee** - The world educates anyone who does not listen to their mother.

3. **Hihaa ni ughwai** - Intelligence is wealth.

4. **Tabia etuna mahukha** - Character is incurable.

5. **Sambya njukhi ulie rukhi** - Follow the bees and taste its honey.

6. **Suntu neatiuwiya atijiumanya intu** - Who does not ask does not learn.

7. **Omwana wakukhu urumuhanga mwewe** - The prayer of the hen does not affect the eagle.

8. **Neguesong'e gwe nguu, nuwumwe umuthotho** - Unity is strength and division is weakness.

9. **Nuunyokhua ngumi ukuta uguraria mikhono akwe mughonjo** — Whoever hits a wall hurts his fist.

10. **Viata amantu nuguvua somba euja hasira ama somba** — Happiness of the fisherman, anger of the fish.

11. **Naje neahunukha uthuyajoa** - We do not collect water once poured.

12. **Mukhuu abiri bithagikha musee umwe** - Two bulls do not live in one same stable.

13. **Jewahanga nyungu nephea utajughuthe gakhingi** - If you have a new pan do not throw the old one.

14. **Manyanjo ni ikhari udhudahaufiha** - Love is a cough you cannot hide.

15. **Mpampwea ndio mwendo** - He who goes slowly goes surely.

16. **Khusierhea antyi ugwa** - Slipping is not the same as falling.

17. **Khunyofeja atyughataa newaghatoo umanye wahanga** - Whoever seeks does not tire.

18. **Jewanghombifa ughuona meingi** — To live long is to see a lot.

19. **Jiho itikwethi ipazia** - The eyes have no curtain.

20. **Hara hara ethikweti Baraka** - Speed does not bring blessings.

21. **Hintu nirikhwa ryitikhowa** - An investment does not rot.

22. **Hifanda ra mwegheghe nereghu mphei** - The liar's path is very short.

23. **Dafanda abiri amurenye piri** - The two paths confuse the hyena.

24. **Khunyugunyui ugugi'juya gebaba** - Little by little we fill the basket.

25. **Kifanda ne ririfu ritiurya khona** - A long road has no shortage of curves.

TOGOLESE PROVERBS

Country: Togo

Capital City: Lomé

Area of Country: 56,785 km²

Population: 9,107,639

Demonyms: Togolese

Currency: West African Franc (XOF)

Independence Day: 27th April 1960

Official Language: French

National Languages: Ewe, Kabiyé

Other Languages Include: Aja, Gen, Tem, Gourmanchéma, Ifé, Nawdm, Lama, Ntcham, Moba, Kusaal, Mbelime, Wudu, Adangbe, Biali

National Motto: Work, Liberty, Homeland

ABOUT KABIYÉ

Kabiye, also spelled "Kabye" or "Kabiyé," is a Gur language spoken primarily by the Kabye people in the northern region of Togo. Traditionally, Kabiye was not a written language, and it relied on oral transmission. However, efforts have been made to develop a writing system for Kabiye using the Latin script to aid in literacy and education.

KABIYÉ - ENGLISH

1. **Ɖoŋ-tʊ ɛɛwakɩ ajama naalɛ** - Two weak are always stronger than one strong.

2. **Afelaa naɣna ɛma** - It's the wizards who recognize themselves.

3. **Ajama sɔkɪ ɛma kpamla** - The weak always help each other out.

4. **Ajɛya kpɛndɪɣ so aakpɛndɪɣ payɛ** - Same rhythm, different dances.

5. **Aleɣya pɪyɛ kʊ sumaɣ** - A stone thrown at random can kill a bird.

6. **Aminda ɛɛkʊʊ** - Whispers are inoffensive.

7. **Awiya ɛɛcakɪ ɛma yɔɔ** - Two kings do not occupy the same throne.

8. **Caɣ ɖiɣɖiɣ kɛna sɪm kɔyɛ** - Staying calm keeps you out of trouble.

9. **Ɖɪsɛɛ ɛɛkʊʊ you** - Greeting do not kill anybody.

10. **Caɣ taa nɛ sɪm ; wolo taa nɛ sɪm** - Moving or not, death is always there.

11. **Abalʊ ɛɛsɪkɪ tɔm naalɛ** - A man does not die twice.

12. **Ɖa-caa yɔɔdɪ ndʊ yɔ, ndʊ ɖɪtɔkɪ** - We will do everything according to the father's recommendations.

13. **Ɖaahaɣkaɣ kʊyʊmaɣ taa holaa ɛɛñazɪɣ ɖama pɛtɛ pa-taa** - Rats in the same trunk don't have to bite each other.

14. **Ɛyaa naalɛ kaɣ pɪyɛ nɛ pokuli-ɖɪ** - Together, two people can move a rock.

15. **Ɛyaa naalɛ haɣ nasunʊwa** - Only two people pass each other a ladle.

16. **Ɛsɔ tɪna kpɪnɛ (kpɪŋɖɛ) tɛtʊ paɣ huyuu** - The parcel belongs to God; the earth only carries the bag.

17. **Ɛsɪyɛ ñaŋ ɛsɪhuɖuu** - The eye respects the pupil.

18. **Ɖʋm ɛñazı-ŋ ŋna ɛ-lɛsıtʋ ŋseɣ** - Who has already been bitten by the snake will be afraid of its skin.

19. **Ɛsıyɛ ŋɖı ɖına ñɔsı yɔ ŋɖı haɣna mıŋ** - It's the eye that sees the smoke that looks for the flame.

20. **Eleu ɛɛkʋʋ pʋcɔ hayʋ** - The devil does not kill the one who gives first.

21. **Eduuye wiɣna kına-tʋ** - Only a proverb can hurt a shaman.

22. **Ɛsısɛmıyɛ tɛkɛ kewiyaɣ** - Jealousy is not royalty.

23. **Ɛgɔm wɛ ɛzı pıɣa yɔ** - A foreigner is like a child.

24. **Ɛsɔ haɣna cee maatɔɔ we** - Only God provides for tomorrow.

25. **Ɛsɔ ɛɛlakı pʋyʋ titiɖe** - God does nothing by halves.

TUNISI PROVERBS

Country: Tunisia
Capital City: Tunis
Area of Country: 163,610 km²
Population: 12,486,219
Demonyms: Tunisian
Currency: Tunisian Dinar (TND)
Independence Day: 20th March 1956
Official Language: Arabic
Other Languages Include: Tunisian Arabic, French, Tamazight of
Djerba, Matmata Berber
National Motto: Freedom, Order, Justice

ABOUT TUNISIAN ARABIC

Tunisian Arabic, also known as Tunisian Darija, is a variety of Arabic spoken in Tunisia, a North African country located on the Mediterranean coast. It is the native language of most Tunisians and is used in everyday communication. Loanwords from French, Italian, Spanish, and Turkish are integrated into the language, due to historical interactions and trade relations.

TUNISIAN ARABIC – ENGLISH

1. إلّي خْلق ما يْضيّع - The one who creates will not let you get lost.
2. إضْحك للدِّنْيا تِضْحكّلك - Laugh, and life will laugh with you.
3. البل تمشي على كبارها - Camels follow their elders.

154

4. دْخول الحمّام موش كي خُروجو - Entering the Hammam is not like leaving it.

5. إلّي ما تعرفش تشطح اتقول الأرض عوجة - She who does not know how to dance, will say that the floor is sloping.

6. هُرب مِن قطْرة جا تَحْت ميزاب - He fled a drop and found himself under a rain gutter.

7. الغريق ما يهمو مطر - A drowned person does not care about rain.

8. كي اتّطيح البقْرة تُكْثُر سْكاكِنْها - When the cow falls, knives appear around it.

9. يْمين البكّوش في صِدْرو - The mute's oath is in his chest.

10. الفم المغلوق ما تدخله ذبّانة — A fly cannot open a closed mouth.

11. أعْمِل روحِك مهْبول تْعيش - Pretend to be a fool and you will live.

12. اسْمع الكَلام إلّي يْبكّيك وْ ما تِسْمعْش الكَلام إلّي يْضحّكك - Listen to the words that make you cry and do not listen to those that make you laugh.

13. كان صاحبك عسل ما تلحسوش الكلّو - If your friend is honey, do not lick him thoroughly.

14. الفْلوس وْسخ الدِنْيا - Money is the rubbish of life.

15. ما يْحِس بالجمْرة كان الّي يعْفِس عْليها - Only he who walks on embers can feel it.

16. حتى القطوسة تخبش على روحها - Even the cat scratches to defend itself.

17. عقل النساء زينهم وزين الرجال عقلهم - A woman's intelligence is her beauty and a man's beauty is his intelligence.

18. الاعور في بلاد العميان سلطان - The one-eyed person among the blind is a king.

19. لي يحب اللولو يسهر الليل كلو - He who desires pearls stays up all night long.

20. الفهيم من غمزه والبهيم من همزه - The intelligent person understands from a wink and the donkey needs to be prodded.

21. إسْأل مْجرّب وْ ما تِسْألْش طْبيب - Ask someone experienced; do not ask a doctor.

22. إلّي عْطى كِلْمْتو عْطى رقْبْتو - He who gave his word, gave his neck.

23. إذا نصْحِك التاجر راهو شْطر النّصيحة ليه - When a trader gives you advice, half of the advice is for him.

24. خْبل الكِذْب قْصير وخبل الصّدْق طْويل - The rope of lying is short, and the rope of truth is long.

25. كان الكِذب يْنجّي، الصّدْق أنْجى - If lying saves, then telling the truth saves more.

UGANDAN PROVERBS

Country: Uganda
Capital City: Kampala
Area of Country: 241,038 km²
Population: 48,933,006
Demonym: Ugandan
Currency: Ugandan Shilling (UGX)
Independence Day: 9ᵗʰ October 1962
Official Languages: English, Swahili
Other Languages Include: Kiga, Luganda, Adhola, Kuman, Soo, Runyankore, Bari, Lango, lk, Rutooro, Alur, Acholi, Karamojong, Lusoga
National Motto: For God and My Country

ABOUT KIGA

Kiga, also known as Chiga, Rukiga or Ruchiga, is a Bantu language spoken by the Kiga people primarily in southwestern Uganda, particularly in the Kigezi subregion.

KIGA – ENGLISH

1. **Tura owomuntu okusingaho kutura omwitagyi ryekiti -** Take shelter in a person rather than in a tree branch.

2. **Okukora hamwe nibwo burugo bwa amani -** Working together is the source of strength.

3. **Otakayehutzya okuhaburwa kwomwana** - Do not ignore a child's advice.

4. **Omutabani nabonabona ahabwebibi byishewe** - The son suffers because of his father's sins.

5. **Omuntu arikukukyira aryaguma nakukyira** - A person who is older than you always remain older.

6. **Omuzengyerezi arikuruga omuka akaza omundijo nibamushuka ebyizi bigubire** - He who roams from home to home get dirty water spattered on his face.

7. **Omuchezi takagaruka omuka nengaro nsha** - The early person does not go home empty-handed.

8. **Okukuraganisa ekyihuro kyihango nabasa kukwisa enjara** - He who promises you a bigger share may starve you to death.

9. **Tuyembe tigukagwa haare nekiti kyagwe** — Better to stumble in your steps than to stumble in your mouth.

10. **Omunwa murungi niguza kukuyamba kurya nomugabe** - A good mouth will make you eat with a king.

11. **Okukurisa naba nakutegyeka** - He who feeds you controls you.

12. **Okubuza tibushema** - Asking is not stupidity.

13. **Okurime ekyina namaririza ariwe akyirimu** - A person who digs a hole ends up in the same hole.

14. **Oyanza wayeyerera enju yawe otakagyire kugamba eyabandi okweteyerire** - Two cocks must not cook in one pot.

15. **Embwa tekumoka ekaruma** - A dog cannot bark and bite at the same time.

16. **Bayine abaana namara ekiro aha muhanda** - No one despises his own tobacco however bad it may be.

17. **Banza wayeyerera enju yawe otakagyire kugamba eyabandi okweteyerire** - First sweep your own house before you despise someone else's.

18. **Burimuntu nayegura omugamba gwe** - Each person bears his own burden.

19. **Amihande ebiri ekabuzabuza empisi** - Shyness killed the hare in its den.

20. **Ekyibakugurize nibabasa kukyikwaka kandi okyakyenda** - What is loaned to you can be taken from you even when you still need it.

21. **Owayesigyire obugiga bwamukuruweye akafa obworo** - The one who relied on his brother's wealth died poor.

22. **Nikirungi kutandiika nobworo kusinga okutandika nobugiga** - It is better to begin with poverty rather than riches.

23. **Nomanya akaze komuntu omubwire bwenjara** - You know someone's true character during famine.

24. **Okurinza okukora, okwo okukora nikugaruka kumurinda** - He who delays actions, that action always awaits him.

25. **Okwenda kuziina nabanza yatera engoma** - He who wants to dance must starts beating the drums.

ZAMBIAN PROVERBS

Country: Zambia

Capital City: Lusaka

Area of Country: 752,614km ^{2}

Population: 20,697,876

Demonym: Zambian

Currency: Zambian Kwacha (ZMW)

Independence Day: 24th October 1964

Official Language: English

Other Languages Include: Bemba, Chewa (Nyanja), Tonga, Tumbuka, Nsenga

National Motto: One Zambia, One Nation

ABOUT BEMBA

Bemba is a Bantu language spoken in Zambia. Bemba is primarily spoken in the Copperbelt Province, the Northern Province, and parts of the Luapula Province in Zambia. It is also spoken by some communities in neighbouring countries, such as the Democratic Republic of Congo and Tanzania.

BEMBA – ENGLISH

1. **Akanwa ka mwefu takabepa** – The bearded mouth does not lie.

2. **Umukulu tapusa kebo apusa kabwe** – An elder may miss his target when throwing a stone but he does not miss wisdom.

3. **Umweni wa kolwe alya ifyo kolwe alyako** – The visitor of the monkey eats what the monkey eats.

4. **Umwana wa mupeta fuaku nsala** - The child of a generous person never starves.

5. **Lesa mufushi tafulila umo** – God is not a smith who works for one person only.

6. **Uwa iketepabili afwile kumenshi** - Indecisiveness is not good in life.

7. **Nang'ombe pa bana taya** – A cow never runs away from her calves.

8. **Ukuboko bapota ukumine** – It is a stubborn arm that is twisted.

9. **Insala ya mubiyo taifufya tulo** – Your neighbour's hunger does not keep you awake.

10. **Akatondo ka bwalwa ni nsokolola twebo** – A calabash of beer reveals a lot of hidden things

11. **Umulilo wa mfumu taucepa** – The fire of the chief is never too small.

12. **Ifyakulya ubushiku bafimwena kumalushi** - What you eat in the darkness will be seen in your vomit.

13. **Kolwe uwakota asabilwa na bana** – When a monkey is old she is fed by her sons.

14. **Umwana wamusha afundilwa apafundilwa umwana wanfumu** - The child of slaves is educated where the king's child gets lessons.

15. **Kwimba kati kusansha na Lesa** - To dig a root is to mix with God.

16. **Umucele ukufina kumfwa kubasenda** — The weight of a bag of salt is only felt by those who carry it.

17. **Abali babili na mano yabili** — Where there are two people there is double wisdom.

18. **Ubushiku usheme ne cimbala ciloca** — The day you are unlucky, even cold left over from the previous night can burn you.

19. **Lesa talombwa nama alombwo mweo** — From God one does not ask for meat but for life.

20. **Wanya wanya tateke calo** — Threats and insults never rule a country.

21. **Ululumbi lwamulanda kukakata** - One who is poor will only improve their status by working hard.

22. **Mwenda mfula taceba kwiulu** - One who journeys during the time of rains does not look to the skies.

23. **Tabatuka ngwena elyo taulayabuka umumana** - We do not insult the crocodile before crossing the river.

24. **Uwabingwa ukowate minina** - One who intends to swim does not just stand.

25. **Uwa kwensha bushiku bamutasha elyo bwacha** - One who makes you walk at night is thanked when it is day.

ZIMBABWEAN PROVERBS

Country: Zimbabwe

Capital City: Harare

Area of Country: 390,745km ^{2}

Population: 16,732,569

Demonym: Zimbabwean

Currency: United States Dollar (USD)

Independence Day: 18th April1980

Official Languages: English, Shona, Chewa, Chibarwe, Kalanga, Sotho, Koisan, Nambya, Ndau, Ndebele, Shangani, Tonga, Tswana, Venda, Xhosa

Other Languages Include: Chilapalapa, Kunda, Tsoa, Tswa, Lozi, Tjwao

National Motto: Unity, Freedom, Work

ABOUT SHONA

Shona is a Bantu language spoken by the Shona people primarily in Zimbabwe. It is also spoken by minorities in neighbouring countries, such as Mozambique, Zambia, and Botswana. Shona has several dialects, with Zezuru often considered the standard dialect.

SHONA – ENGLISH

1. **Miromo ya vanhu haiwire pasi** – The words of men do not fall.

2. **Kurayira ndokurajira anonzwa, kurayisa asanganzwi ku udza ibwe** – You give advice to one who listens, to give advice to one who does not listen is like telling a stone to do something.

3. **Kafamba huona** – Travelling is seeing.

4. **Mugoni wepwere ndaasinayo** – He who can deal with children is he who has none.

5. **Mukuru haafandanurwi hapwa** - An elder does not reveal the secrets of the village.

6. **Kukurukura hunge wapotswa** – You can only tell the tale when you have survived it.

7. **Kakara kununa hudya kamwe** – Success comes by the help of others.

8. **Usarove nyoke uchisiya runhenda** - Do not kill a snake and leave its tail.

9. **Chembere mukadzi hazvienzani nekurara mugota** - Poor quality is better than nothing.

10. **Kuvunduka chati kwatara hunge uine katurike** – To be upset by the rumours going round means you know something about them.

11. **Kure kwe meso nzeve dzinonzwa** – Out of sight the ears still hear.

12. **Mwana kuberekwa vaviri, mugota hamuchemi kacheche** - Some things cannot be done by one person alone, like conceiving a child.

13. **Pasi panodya zvakakomba** – The earth consumes that which is precious.

14. **Izwi remurwere ngerine nyaya** – The word of a sick man is very important.

15. **Zvina manenji kuti gudo ripunzike mumuti** – It is most extraordinary to hear that a baboon has fallen from a tree.

16. **Uchayenka bako wanaiwa** – You will remember the cave when you are wet.

17. **Kandiro kanoenda kunobva kamwe** - Favours go to those who have given them before.

18. **Chinokura chichirwa ingwe, kwete munhu kuyaza** – It is not a quarrelsome man but a leopard that thrives on fighting.

19. **Chakavanza mbayo matenga** – What hides the tip of the rooftree is the roof.

20. **Muromo ibako unozvidyiviria** – The mouth is a cave, it protects itself.

21. **Mvura yateuka haichina muhoreri** – Split water has nobody to gather it up.

22. **Rutaro mwena, kutevedza huguma** – Pleasure is like a mouse hole; if you follow it, you come to its end.

23. **Kwagwera mtengo wanthambi sikusowa** - Where a tree with branches has fallen is known by everybody.

24. **Tsapata rukukwe hazvienzani nokuvata pasi** – Sleeping on an old sleeping mat is not as bad as sleeping on the ground.

25. **Kudzidza hakuperi** - Education is a continuous perpetual process.

A NOTE FROM
MOTHERLAND LITERAURE

Preserving African Culture, One Book At A Time.

As you reach the end of this book, we want to thank you for taking this journey with us into the world of African proverbs. It has been an honour to share this collection with you, and we hope it has enriched your understanding of the profound wisdom that Africa holds.

We encourage you to carry these proverbs with you and share them with those you care about. Engage in discussions, reflect on their meanings, and find ways to apply their wisdom in your own life. By doing so, you contribute to the preservation of African culture and the continuation of the oral tradition that has sustained these proverbs for centuries.

If this book has resonated with you, we kindly ask that you consider sharing it with others who might benefit from its insights. Your support is deeply appreciated.

Lastly, we invite you to leave a review or share your thoughts on this book. Your feedback is instrumental in helping us reach more readers and continue our mission of preserving African culture.

Thank you for being a part of this journey, and we hope these proverbs continue to inspire and guide you in the years to come.

The Motherland Literature Team

NOTES

NOTES

SPECIAL BONUS

Want this bonus book for <u>free?</u>

Get <u>FREE</u> unlimited access to this and all our new books by joining our community!

SCAN w/ your camera TO JOIN!

Printed in Great Britain
by Amazon

47524823R00096